Property Investment Mastery

A Foolproof Property Investment Framework
To Help You Maximise Your Profits

Vittorio G Fierro

Disclaimer

This book is designed to provide information and motivation to our readers. It is sold with the understanding that the author and publisher are not engaged to render any type of psychological, legal, or any other kind of professional advice. The content is the sole expression and opinion of its author. Neither the publisher nor the individual author(s) shall be liable for any physical, psychological, emotional, financial, or commercial damages, including, but not limited to, special, incidental, consequential or other damages. Our views and rights are the same: You are responsible for your own choices, actions, and results.

The content of the book is solely written by the author.

DVG STAR Publishing are not liable for the content of the book.

Published by DVG STAR PUBLISHING

www.dvgstar.com
email us at info@dvgstar.com

NO PART OF THIS WORK MAY BE REPRODUCED OR STORED IN AN INFORMATIONAL RETRIEVAL SYSTEM WITHOUT THE EXPRESS PERMISSION OF THE PUBLISHER IN WRITING.

ISBN: 1-912547-61-9
ISBN-13: 978-1-912547-61-6

DEDICATION

I would like to dedicate this book to my parents, who not only established our family-owned Sales and Lettings Agency back in 1980 and have been a massive part of the success it has achieved, helping hundreds of thousands of clients over those years with their property needs but had also created the platform of a 'ready-made' and successful business for me to come into. They have given me the guidance and support that I greatly required to help me realise the importance of having strong core values as well as helping me to develop a keen desire for success in my own life. Thanks to their 'never give up and always strive for perfection' attitude, that principle has been firmly instilled into my mind, which is now with me in any and every challenge I face. I am eternally grateful for the sacrifices they have made, quite literally giving up their own lives to ensure that my sister and I have had the benefit of every valuable opportunity in ours. Without their love, guidance, support and persistence, then simply put, I would not be where I am or the person I am today, and so I could not have wished for better parents.

My dedication also extends to my sister, who since becoming part of the organisation has quite literally become the backbone through her determination and commitment to maintaining the high standards set by our parents all those years ago. She is a shining example for many; I am proud to be her brother. I must also mention Sally Lawson, who, without her teachings, this book would not have been possible. She is an inspiration to the Lettings Industry. Her forward and proactive thinking, through which I have been inspired by and learnt from, has helped me to weather the ever-changing climate of the private rental sector by guiding me to making the essential investments into the business, from installing organisational structures and procedures to staff training and development, ensuring that our company's desire and commitment to offering the highest levels of efficient and personable service can be fulfilled.

My coach and Mentor, Tosin Ogunnusi, has truly inspired me always to believe in myself, and through that, I have learnt the secrets to achieving all that I desire. Through his teachings, he has enabled me to completely change my view on life, and I now fully understand the importance of always pushing yourself out of your comfort zone if you truly wish to accomplish your dreams. He has helped me become a Professional Public Speaker, which has been my burning desire for as long as I can remember. As a result, I now regularly present to large audiences with confidence in my ability to teach, help and inspire others, something I had never really believed I could achieve. I have learnt that in life, you're either 'on your way or in the way', and I realise this more and more as I open my mind up to what can be accomplished when we believe in ourselves. Thank you, Tosin, for all that you have given me. You are a truly amazing and inspiring person. In a world full of hidden dangers and uncertainties, you are a shining light representing all that is good. You are hope, clarity, and belief, and I owe so much to you.

My dedication would not be complete without mentioning my beautiful and loving wife and two adorable children, who have given me the foundation and purpose in life to achieve the very best that I can for them. They are my sunshine on a gloomy day, my motivation and inspiration, and I would be nothing without them.

CONTENTS

"Opportunities don't happen, you create them."
— Chris Grosser

FOREWORD

For many, the idea of property investing may seem like a desirous route to increasing your personal income. 'Get-rich-quick' schemes seem to abound by the hundreds from so-called 'property gurus', and for most, with property courses costing tens of thousands of pounds, most likely filled with jargon and bravado, it may seem hard to know who to trust and where to start.

For people like me who have spent their careers in the property world, these 'get-rich-quick' property gurus, at the minimum, make us roll our eyes and sigh in frustration. But for the most part, they make us concerned for the countless newbie investors who are likely being duped into parting with their thousands for information they could just as easily get from seasoned letting agents who not only know well the pitfalls to avoid but who can spot a good property investment at 60 paces.

Suppose you're someone who is interested in investing in property. In that case, you may find yourself looking for an easy-to-read guide which will explain these pitfalls, help you with the big decisions you will need to make and, most importantly, provide you with tangible benefits that you could make from joining the property investment world.

If that is what you're looking for, I'm pleased to let you know you've found it.

Vittorio Fierro's guide to property investing goes against the grain of most property investment books and courses; there's no jargon, no over-complication, and no TV personalities boasting about how they made their fortune. Instead, each section has been concisely examined and explained, taking the investor from the very start of their property journey through each defined step of market forces, finance and then onto letting the property.

Becoming a property investor can certainly be a lucrative decision many have jumped into with two feet. Since the late eighties, our Private rented sector in the UK has boomed, going from only 8% of homes in 1988 to over 20% privately rented in 2021. The driver for this was the 1988 Housing Act which was a watershed moment for the UK rental market. It handed much more power to Landlords than they had previously enjoyed, and it was a bold leap, moving away from restrictive tenancies like Rent Act 1977 tenancies and becoming illustrative of the ideals of the Thatcher government towards greater free-market autonomy in the rented housing sector.

Throughout this book, Vito (as he likes to be called by family and friends) imparts his knowledge logically, providing a sound analysis of the different types of property investors, the different high-risk and low-risk investment types and why it pays to diversify your investments over several different property types to lower your risk. This is often something I find many seasoned Landlords fail to identify, falling into a rut of always being an HMO investor, for example.

Later in the book, it's great to see the author explain the concept of leveraging across multiple properties, as I find many Landlords are too intent on buying with just cash, not understanding that purchasing one unencumbered property for £200,000 will only give you one rental income. However, splitting this £200,000 across several properties could give you three or even four rental incomes, thus increasing the monetary amount you receive each month and reducing the risk of losing all rental income from a single void. Of course, there is also greater capital appreciation from four properties than from one.

Although Vito explains the benefits of this, he continuously also analyses the risks and is upfront about these to his readers. It's not often you see this careful explanation of the risks involved rather than the shouty 'buy, leverage, buy' approach we usually see from others.

Finally, a point I find many Landlords forget about is the final step of choosing a good agent with an all-encompassing and experienced service level. We often forget that not everyone understands this valuable insider knowledge that many of us Agents have around the end point management of a tenancy. Vito explains the reasons why cheap agents are definitely never worth it, the detail needed in the systematisation of managing a rental property and the very thorough process that should be undertaken every single time when it comes to finding you the best possible tenants. Because when it comes to letting agents, who look after probably your largest asset, the saying 'buy cheap, buy twice' is never more prevalent.

It's clear that throughout this book, the theme of having a strategy is key, as without a clear strategy for any investment, you are unlikely to be able to effectively measure its success or ensure you can make an agile side-step when things go wrong. Part of your investment strategy should be reading this book with a notepad and pen to take down as many notes as possible. It contains many hidden gems of information that most letting agents will guard closely for fear of revealing their secrets. This makes it invaluable for both seasoned property pros and new investors alike, as what one Landlord may have experienced just once, you can bet a letting agent has experienced hundreds of times. This knowledge and experience that Vito has gained from being a property professional for more than the last two decades are expertly demonstrated and simply given.

I'm confident that reading Vito's book will leave you feeling clearer about your property investment goals and will make your investment journey smoother and more profitable in the long run. After all, an easy 'no hassle' investment with a great yield is the ideal that all of us investors are ultimately always looking for.

Angharad Trueman
Vice President ARLA Propertymark

"Look what everyone else is doing and then go in the opposite direction."
— Warren Buffett

VITTORIO G FIERRO

Having personally worked in the Real Estate Industry since 1999 as part of a family business which my parents started in 1980, I've developed a real understanding and not to mention 'Passion' for property.

I own and manage my own property portfolio, which I started to put together back in 2006 and use the knowledge I have gained over the years to help other Property Investors gain the financial freedom they desire. In addition, I am a Professional Public Speaker and regularly contribute to TV and Radio news broadcasts sharing my knowledge and opinions on the Real Estate Industry.

It has always been important to me to be able to help others. As such, I was formerly Chairman of a local Association, which I was a part of setting up to help youngsters feel part of their community. Through our company, I continually support Circus Star Childrens' Charity.

WHO ARE WE?

As an Independent, family-owned and run Estate and Letting Agency, City & County have served the Peterborough and surrounding market since 1980. During this time, we've helped 1000s of clients with guidance on Buy to Let Investment strategies and sourcing suitable properties to tailor specific requirements. We have also let well over 7000 properties worth over £600m in value and £3.5m in rent, and we currently manage around £540m worth of property for our Landlord clients whilst also having sold over 15,000 properties in our years of business equating to over £2b in value.

The Lettings side of the business is headed by me, which I've been part of since 1999 following my graduation from University. At this point, I had decided to become part of the family organisation. During this time, I have developed a great understanding and wealth of knowledge, having started at the very bottom, learning all aspects of Tenancy Management and combining that with the presence of the Sales side of the company, where I've developed those skills to better serve Investor clients by understanding how to maximise their investment opportunities.

I've managed to create cohesion between the Sales and Lettings departments, encouraging both sides to work together, enabling our Investors to benefit from the in-house opportunities that we're then able to present.

WHY IS REAL ESTATE SUCH AN IMPORTANT INVESTMENT?

Investing in real estate is a way to protect against inflation. With high inflation, your rental income and property value would skyrocket, so without such investment; your cash flow would decrease as the cost of living rises.

Investing in real estate is a great method to diversify an investment portfolio. The stock market correlates poorly with real estate, and home prices are significantly less volatile than equities. Property owners can also benefit from a variety of tax incentives, which increase the return on investment.

Finally, building a portfolio of rental properties in geographically diverse places makes investors more resilient and capable of weathering all types of economic storms.

There are different types of real estate investing, just as there are various types of real estate assets (commercial real estate, single-family rental property, apartment buildings, real estate wholesaling, real estate debt, and others).

The method that would be considered most suitable to a particular investor should be determined by criteria such as their risk tolerance, how much control they want over the asset, whether they are a novice or an expert in real estate investing, how much cash they have for a deposit payment, and the level of cash flow they seek.

With the extent of knowledge that I have accumulated over the years with our tested and proven methodologies, I have created a unique framework known as my "Time-tested and proven property investment profit system" that should help to guide you in the right direction. This is all about maximising your return on profit. This book will cover a range of solutions that will help you overcome the many challenges that Landlords face. It has been collated into a simple and easy-to-understand format so that you can get started on your Investment journey straight away.

There are over 170 pieces of legislation in the Private Rental Sector today, so ensuring that you (and more so your property investment) are fully compliant within the areas they cover is essential because ignorance is not a defence should you find yourself on the wrong side of Tenancy Law. Remember, your responsibility as a Landlord is to provide safe, habitable accommodation for your Tenants, including anyone else who should come into the property, as well as pets. As a Letting Agency, we cover every aspect of full Tenancy Management, working to ensure that Landlords' property investment is let and maintained to an appropriate standard whilst also maximizing its return on that investment. Professional Tenancy Management is by no means straightforward, especially given the ever-changing landscape of Governmental intervention. Therefore, your choice of Lettings Agency to look after your property investment should be carefully considered. How are *we* different? Why do *we* do it the way we do, and why should *you* do it this way? As a reputable and long-standing Sales and Lettings Agency, I wanted to create the "Time-tested and proven property investment profit system" to show you exactly what is required. My overall aim is to help you build a safe, secure and profitable portfolio that gives you longevity.

So, let's get started. As you can see, the framework has been split into three categories of Sourcing, Increases and Agents. We will be covering each individual topic within our chapters in more detail using my unique framework for each division.

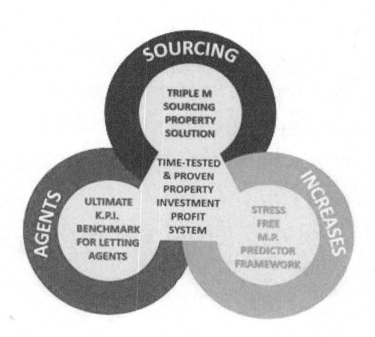

"Develop your assets before your liabilities. Your home is a liability. It will always cost you money and never return you money. Buy your assets first, then when you have enough of these you can use your assets to buy your liabilities, i.e. your home, cars and holidays"
- Robert Kyosaki
Author of Rich Dad, Poor Dad

TRIPLE M SOURCING PROPERTY SOLUTION ™

"Success in real estate starts when you
believe you are worthy of it."
~ Michael Ferrara

What is property sourcing for investors?

Finding the ideal property or properties for your investment can be difficult. Family responsibilities and day jobs probably take up the majority of your time, and things become even more challenging if you're new to real estate investing, spending a lot of time managing the properties in your current portfolio, or looking to buy a new property in a location you're not very familiar with.

A reputable property sourcing agency can be a massive help in this kind of situation. A service like this essentially means that someone else will handle all of the labour-intensive work for you; all you have to do is put pen to paper when required. Do you have questions regarding property sourcing and whether it might be a good option for your upcoming real estate investment? Then read on.

There are several distinct kinds of property sourcers. Some operate as independent consultants, certain property sourcing agencies employ some, and others are employed by real estate and property investment firms.

A dedicated specialist will perform the majority of the

work to identify a suitable property for you when you use a property sourcing service, as we have already explained. To present you with the most promising properties for your consideration, they will search the local real estate market and look for any attractive 'off-market deals'. Additionally, they'll carry out all required due diligence investigations, bargain with the seller to get a favourable agreement and prepare all required documentation for your signature.

Naturally, we always advise that you double-check everything your property sourcer tells you about a possible investment property and not just accept their word for it.

Check to see if the bargain they have found for you is genuinely competitive compared to the typical price of properties in the area, and ask them what factors they considered when predicting your ROI. Check to see if the property's predicted rental yield is consistent with the rents that are typically posted in the neighbourhood.

Simply put, you must complete your homework. This entails exercising due diligence and running a background check. Get specific information by asking them about previous transactions they have undertaken. If feasible, seek recommendations or testimonials from previous clients, or attempt to speak with them directly.

A reliable property sourcer won't object if you do your research and raise the appropriate questions. Additionally, they'll be happy to give you any information you might need. However, it is typically a bad sign if they are elusive and cagey.

Never sign anything before reviewing it by a Solicitor, especially regarding property matters.

As you can see, even though working with a property sourcer makes things simpler for you, you should still double-check the numbers given to you because investing in real estate requires a significant financial commitment.

Now, this is what we do to help our clients with sourcing.

The 3 steps for real estate sourcing

How to find fresh prospects is one of the first queries most commercial real estate investors ask. Unfortunately, there isn't a straightforward, one-step solution; rather, it depends on several factors that, taken together, might serve as a general rule of thumb for the real estate industry. However, once you've mastered these simple procedures, you'll have access to a limitless supply of investment opportunities that can generate a consistent flow of deals. Therefore, I've combined these three steps into my "Triple M Sourcing property solution" to help you understand it in a more simplified form.

The three M's are:

- Manoeuvre
- Market
- Money

"When we start earning, where most of us go wrong is that we spend first and then save what we have left. What we should be doing is saving (investing) first and then spending what's left instead."
- Robert Kyosaki

Manoeuvre (Strategy)

The strategy behind property investment is important when looking to ensure that your asset is making the returns you intended. For this reason, it is strongly recommended that you start your investment journey with education via a Buy to Let specialist. This is not to be confused with those in the market who have developed their own techniques that they then want to encourage you to adopt. Property Investment should be right for YOU. What is important is to establish through Investment education that various strategies are available to you. So what needs to come out of your education is that you yourself identify what type of Landlord you are or intend to be and, therefore, which strategy works best for you. From that, the intention is that you are then able to identify what type of property you should be buying and where to attract the type of tenants you want to achieve the intended ROI.

What Sort of Investor am I?

Before investing in property, you must consider what sort of investor you are. Answer the questions below, and you should be able to identify YOUR ideal Investment.

- Are you a high-risk or low-risk investor?
- Are you seeking capital appreciation or income?
- If capital, do you want it immediately or in the long term?
- If you are looking for Income, do you want high-income "active" or medium-income "passive"?

- What sum of money do you have available now?
- Are you experienced in DIY or have contacts in the trade?
- Do you want to build a portfolio that will be self-funding?
- Do you own any existing properties that you want to form part of your portfolio now?

Risk Assessments

Investors need to consider what type of Landlord they are or would like to be, i.e. high risk or low risk? High risk will result in more hands-on Tenancy Management based on the type of Tenant that the property you choose and the set-up of the property, is likely to attract. Low risk would be the more desirable Tenant, i.e. Professional, with a lesser chance of issues in any form.

There are many things to think about when letting out a property, regardless of whether you are considering making your first buy-to-let investment or you are an experienced portfolio Landlord. It can all seem quite overwhelming at the best of times. And so our Property Sourcing service, combined with our Full Tenancy Management service (which I'll explain in further detail in chapter 3), is designed to take care of all of that so that you can go about your daily tasks in the meantime. We recognise that as a Landlord, you have a number of significant strategic goals that you would like to accomplish, such as;

- earning the highest return possible on your investment(s)
- controlling risk
- minimising void periods

You must reach a goal level of rental income and longer-term capital growth to maximise the return on your investment. However, maximising return is not achieved by accident but rather a result of using a method that is thoroughly thought out and put into practice, such as;

- choosing the appropriate property in the appropriate location
- spending the right amount to keep the property in good condition.
- achieving the appropriate rent amount.
- securing and keeping the ideal tenant
- reducing void/vacant times.
- reducing your risk exposure.

You have the freedom to choose who you wish to let your property to (within reason, of course). Additionally, you have the freedom to refuse to let to whomever you choose (again within reason). International businesses invest millions in setting up systems to check out potential employees. This is due to the fact that they are aware of the potential financial consequences of recruiting the wrong type of candidate. Even if your budget isn't a million pounds, you should categorise your tenants into high-risk and low-risk groups to not jeopardise your profitability.

However, you must adhere to these four rules while conducting tenant screening from an investment standpoint.

- Rule #1: You must conduct the most exhaustive references feasible, including credit checks, earnings verification, Right to Rent checks (a criminal offence if you get this part wrong) and past Landlord references. You should hire a specialist to assist you with this, as it is imperative that you get this part of the procedure right.
- Rule #2: Take your time. Rushed decisions could cost you thousands of pounds if you end up selecting the wrong Tenant
- Rule #3. Be sure to ask questions about the nature of the prospective Tenant's proposed rental, i.e. why they are looking to rent, how long they are planning

to reside in your property, whether their circumstances are likely to change in the future and what impact that may have on the rental, whether anyone else is likely to move in at a later date etc. Asking these kinds of questions at the forefront avoids any unexpected scenarios that you're not then ready for

- Rule #4: Consider a phone interview first, and be harsh about filtering down to the type of Tenant that you want to attract

Survivors of your vigorous filtration are likely to be the kinds of Tenants many Landlords would strive to secure, assuming you followed your four guidelines religiously. Being the diligent, analytical investor that you are, you'll go one step further and classify the risks.

You should consider very carefully the type of market you want to aim at in terms of your prospective tenants' demographics. Whether to consider restrictions on pets and smokers is often a common scenario that runs across a Landlord's mind. The main concerns, of course, are the property's condition and possible damage caused by the animals themselves. That is not to suggest that all pet owners should be kept away from your property investment. Far from it, I personally have experience of many Tenants as pet owners who have carefully looked after their rental properties to the expected standard. By the way, at the time of writing, the UK Government is proposing restrictions on the freedom of choice Landlords may have with regard to allowing pets, so this should be something to bear in mind. Speaking of Government legislation, the recently introduced Tenant Fee Ban in 2019 brought in a cap on the amount of security deposit that a Landlord can charge, which is now five weeks' worth of the value of the rent. A common strategy when allowing pets has often been to take a larger deposit (however, this, of course, is now not possible), and so to counter that limitation, you should now consider offering two rent levels whilst your rental property is marketed to let, i.e. the standard rent and then a 'pets considered at £x per calendar month'. This will be considerably higher, thus providing you with a higher income above the achievable market level which should cover your risk should there be excessive damage over and above what there may have been.

Landlords used to drool over the student tenant market. They go great distances to attend a superior school or University close to your property, and their parents are likely prepared to pay a regular rental stream to ensure that they have a roof over their heads. In actuality, the promise of a consistent Tenancy might be the only advantage of letting to students.

Suppose you talk to a real estate investor with experience in letting to students. In that case, they may likely remember the calls from neighbouring properties following the wild college parties, boisterous music, beer feasts etc. However, you must acknowledge that students probably aren't emotionally developed just yet and that, due to peer pressure, may cause a ruckus in your property/ies.

However, postgraduate students may be low-risk tenants. Low-risk tenants are more retirees, white-collar workers and young couples.

If you are fortunate enough to locate retirees interested in renting, my experience is that they can make for the ideal tenants; however, this is not to imply that Landlords take advantage of them.

Retirees tend to have basic requirements, and as long as those needs are met in a timely manner, they will likely be happy. They tend to behave as though it were their own property. You may even find that most of the time, they take greater care of their home than you would have expected. With a well-conducted and managed Tenancy, you could have a long-term Tenant providing you with a consistent and passive income.

Workers in the white-collar category are in professions that lean more toward the soft skills than the hard talents.

Administrators, secretaries, nurses, bank officers, and virtually anyone working in an office can fall under this category. Typically, people spend so much time working that their home is reduced to a place to sleep. However, these tenants can normally be more independent and trustworthy. They are likely to consistently make their rent payments on time, and their income is reliable. Additionally, they may be more self-conscious and shy away from conflict while maintaining fairness and compassion.

White-collar workers and young couples typically have quite similar profiles. The disadvantage is that as they start a family, they will eventually need a larger home. One of the first large purchases they make after receiving a fortune, aside from a vacation to a resort, is a new home.

You must be astute enough to realise that the list above does not encompass all available tenant kinds. It is not even close, but you should pay attention to them because they are the most typical ones.

Important considerations for your strategy when dealing with tenant-Landlord relationships:

- The majority of tenants merely need the bare necessities. These include things like cleanliness, accessibility, safety, and privacy. Delivering them is your responsibility as a competent and complying Landlord.
- Letting to Tenants who you believe will maximise your investment is your business.
- No matter where any issues may originate, take action to solve them as soon as you encounter them.
- Respect the individuality of your tenants.

Active or Passive Income

It is important to understand the distinctions here and what is involved so that you may decide where your preference is. For example, a higher risk strategy will lead to a more active income which will be a more 'hands-on' experience, whereas a lower risk strategy will create more of a passive income. Of course, it goes without saying that the attractiveness to that higher-risk strategy will likely be a higher income, but you need to understand how much is at risk before you go down that road.

There are, of course, ways to minimise your risk exposure should you select a higher-risk strategy. One method to consider is to purchase as a group of Investors, in which case you may decide to set up a Ltd company. This would be an effective way of sharing the financial burden and the impact from any unfortunate circumstances you may have to deal with. Taking this a step further, you may wish to consider investing in a specialised Investment structure (Limited Liability Company) whereby that company actively handles the sourcing and acquiring of a property whilst you merely invest into the 'company' rather than the 'asset' in which case you would then receive a completely 'hands off' income. Of course, in this scenario, you are completely removed from the property acquisition strategy, so it is clear that you'll have no control over the decisions that will be made at the front end.

Both 'high risk' and 'low risk' strategies have advantages and disadvantages. Each investor should carefully weigh their pros and cons before selecting the one that best suits their personal real estate investment preferences.

Finding, acquiring, and managing a business investment property requires a substantial amount of work. The primary distinction between active and passive real estate investment is who completes this activity.

There are often four factors that motivate responsibility for it:

1. Decisions made by management

In an active real estate investment, a person or group of people directly purchase a property. They, therefore, have total authority over choices made for daily administration. In a more passive income scenario (as briefly mentioned above), individual investors buy shares in an LLC that owns the property in a passive real estate transaction. According to the LLC's organisational structure, a "general partner" controls the asset, while passive investors, referred to as "limited partners," have no say in management choices. They solely offer capital. When picking between an active and passive investment, people should think about their personal inclination for control in the deal.

2. Required Skill Level

It requires a great deal of ability and experiences to analyse the cash flows of rental properties and make daily management decisions intended to maximise investment return. As a result, active investors need to be proficient financial analysts and familiar with the best techniques for property management. Real estate professionals are not always required to be active investors. Instead, they give money to people who find, evaluate, and manage real estate on a full-time basis. These person(s) could be real estate investment trusts, Property Sourcers or Tenancy Management specialist firms like ours. Passive investors receive recurring distributions from the property's rental income as payment for their investment. Individuals should evaluate their capacity to estimate cash flows and make management decisions when deciding whether to engage in an active or passive investment to determine which is most appropriate.

3. Commitment to Time

Finding and managing properties requires a large time investment from active real estate investors. Once more, these investors may be private individuals or specialised businesses. Because everyone else makes all the effort, passive investment does not demand a significant time commitment. Investors should choose the most appropriate alternative based on how much time they have to devote to it when deciding between an active and passive real estate investment.

4. Risk

To be clear, both passive and active real estate investment strategies involve some risk. In an active strategy, the risk is assumed by the investors who buy the property; they receive the entire upside but also bear the entire risk. The risk is still present for passive investors, but it is shared by the general partner and the other participants in the transaction. Thus, each person may be at a slightly lower risk.

In general, it should be noted that every investor has unique investment preferences, goals, risk tolerance, time horizon, and return targets. You must consider these and select the tactic that best suits your requirements.

Which Investment is fit for who?

In general, people with large quantities of investable wealth, a lengthy investment horizon, plenty of time to manage the property personally, and the knowledge and expertise to do so are more likely to benefit from an active real estate investment approach.

On the opposite end of the spectrum, a passive strategy is typically best suited for high-income earners who have the resources to invest but lack the expertise, network, or time to discover, acquire, and manage a rental property on their own, such as Physicians, Solicitors, or architects. These tasks are delegated to a professional organisation.

Both active and passive investment strategies have advantages and disadvantages. The main advantage of an active strategy is that the investor(s) keeps all of the income generated by the asset. They are not required to divide it with any other parties or pay a general partner's fee. Consequently, their returns might be a little bit higher. They also have total control over all property identification, acquisition, and management choices, which some people would find more advantageous than the alternative.

Control and receiving 100% of the profits may sound alluring, but it also implies that investors bear 100% of the risk. There is no one else to share the burden with if the transaction fails; thus, they are solely responsible. Active investors must also perform 100% of the work, including performing their due diligence on the property, resolving maintenance requests, and having the know-how to navigate the complexities of lettings legislation. Active investment is so named because it requires a lot of work and can be very inconvenient.

The advantages and dangers of passive investing resemble those of active real estate investing in many ways.

The main advantage is that investors obtain regular cash payouts without having to do anything. In other words, they enjoy all the benefits of ownership without having to deal with creating a business strategy and daily property management. Additionally, if the property's value rises, passive investors could profit significantly from tax breaks and share in the gains. The drawback is that passive real estate investors are powerless to influence day-to-day decisions about property management. Additionally, the general partner or investment manager can charge a fee for managing the property, which could reduce investor returns.

Again, each strategy has advantages and disadvantages. Therefore, each investor should carefully weigh them and select the strategy that best suits their unique situation.

When deciding between a passive and active investment, those interested in real estate should take into account a variety of criteria, including:

1. Investment capital available

An active strategy typically needs more money because investors are responsible for covering the complete down payment. In partnerships, the required individual sum could be a little lower, but the group still needs to develop it.

2. Time

It is well known that active investments take a lot more time than passive ones. Therefore, people must consider how much time they can commit to managing the property and how much their time is worth.

3. Knowledge

It has also been demonstrated that an active investment necessitates significantly higher operational knowledge. Those that possess it might be better suited for active investment. Those who don't might fare better with a passive approach.

4. Tolerance for risk

Once more, the risk is present in both active and passive techniques. However, it is more focused when taking an active approach. For example, imagine a situation where four partners join forces to buy an apartment complex; in this case, the four partners bear the whole transaction risk. Liken this to a real estate syndication, passive structure, or real estate crowdfunding venture. In such a case, the agreement may involve dozens or even hundreds of investors, distributing the risk among them more evenly.

5. Individual Preferences

Finally, every person has personal tastes. Single-family rentals and the retail asset type may appeal to different people. While some people might desire to be heavily active and directly involved in management choices, others might not.

The best strategy typically becomes clear to most investors when these criteria are considered.

An investment strategy that appears to have grown in popularity with Investors and demand from prospective Tenants is the House of Multiple Occupation model (HMO). This would certainly be considered a more active income as the levels of management are likely to be more complex due to increased levels of legislation, the nature of the Tenancies, the type of Tenants they are likely to attract and the higher levels of upkeep, especially to communal areas.

Utility bills (including Broadband and TV license), periodic cleaners and gardener must be factored into HMOs and so fluctuating costs will have a massive bearing on HMOs.

The location of your property investment is also an important factor to consider, as this will have a bearing on the type of tenant it is likely to attract and, of course, the level of rent its likely to achieve. So, is it close to or accessible to major workplaces, e.g. hospitals (which would attract doctors or nurses)?

Dependent on the type of Tenancy, i.e. single lets, company lets or HMOs, there are varying types of legislation which must be adhered to. Certain Local Authorities also run 'Selective Licensing' schemes, adding additional layers of legislation, procedures and compliance that must be adhered to. Take a look at this link which details the Selective Licensing scheme in Peterborough, where I am based; https://www.peterborough.gov.uk/residents/housing/selective-licensing

The type of property purchased will also have a bearing on the levels of maintenance and upkeep required, i.e. older properties are likely to require more work (however, older properties can tend to be larger and more spacious, thus proving more attractive to tenants and commanding a higher rent).

Is this a long-term or short-term plan? This will also have a bearing on what you should buy and at what price.

Dependent on your Investment strategy, you may prefer a higher rental yield or capital appreciation. You won't achieve high levels of both, though, as it doesn't work that way. The Capital Cash Flow Calculator (see the diagram below) is a system that I use as part of our 'Buy to Let Advisory service' that we offer to our clients, which teaches the main principles and strategies of property Investment. It helps an investor determine where they would ideally like to pitch their strategy and how their choice of property based on type, location, and set-up correlates. The diagram demonstrates how capital appreciation and yield work and differ based on the type of property you purchase, the set-up of the Tenancy and where it is located. First, let's take the town or city where you're located. The line across the middle, starting from the left, represents the worst area within that location.

We're talking about where the least desirable neighbourhood is, and property prices are amongst the cheapest. Crime rates will be high, and anti-social behaviour will undoubtedly be common. Crossing to the far-right-hand side of that line will represent the most desirable area for your location, and property prices will be the highest. Next, take the middle of that line and select where you think would be mid-range for your area. As you'll see from the diagram, above the horizontal line represents the level of capital appreciation, and the area below that line represents yield. The next thing you need to do is find out what the average capital appreciation is for properties in your area. Try to base this on over twenty years to get a more reliable figure. In my diagram, you can see that I have worked out that the average rate of capital appreciation for properties across the board in Peterborough over the last twenty years is 6.6%, according to HM Land Registry House Price Index as of Dec 2021. That figure is then placed at the mid-point of the horizontal line. So next, starting at the far left of that line, you then think about the type of property you are likely to find in that area and what you're likely to want to buy. You may be looking at a cheap and rundown four-bedroom terraced property that you then look to refurbish and convert to a six-bed HMO, for example. So here, your yield will be high based on the levels of rent you'll be generating against the likely purchase price. However, the level of capital appreciation (growth in the value of that property) is expected to be low due to the impact that the low quality of the area is likely to have on that investment. Switching to the far right then, here you'll likely be looking at a four or five-bedroom property typically, which is going to have a high level of capital appreciation thanks to the exclusivity of the area that it is located in; however, due to the high purchase price, although the rent is likely to be significantly higher than what you may generate from the left-hand side of that line, the yield will suffer and likely be very low based on the high purchase price. Focusing on the mid-range of that line, you'll be hitting the average capital appreciation for your area. Your rental yield will also be average, so there is a balance between the two. So you can see how the diagram helps show the correlation between capital appreciation and yield as you move across the middle line. Now all that remains is for you to decide where you want to focus your positioning on the horizontal line. The likelihood is that you'll decide, like the majority of Investors I work with, to pitch somewhere around the middle so that you get the 'best of both worlds regarding capital appreciation and yield.

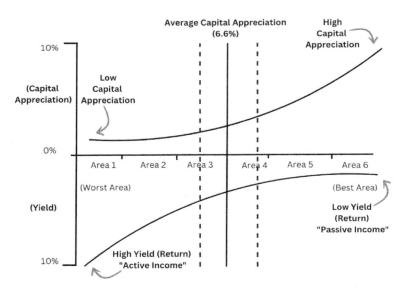

If your strategy involves purchasing multiple properties, some Investors make mistakes such that they put all of their eggs into one basket, i.e. they buy the same type of property in the same area off the back of the good performance of an earlier property. However, what must really be considered is the effects of a sudden or gradual change of circumstance to that area that then may subsequently affect that property's performance (nightmare neighbours down the road making life misery for nearby residents, local authority builds a busy road nearby causing noise from traffic or passes plans to build a large development of properties making the area more overcrowded). Perhaps that particular type of property is no longer flavour of the month for whatever reason (flats have long been considered a popular choice for investors as tenants like the low maintenance aspect, especially as there is no garden to maintain; however, look how the Covid pandemic affected peoples' opinions of living with shared communal areas). The point here is that it pays to consider different types of properties in different areas to spread the risk.

Finding deals in real estate can be one of the toughest obstacles for those just entering the market, and without taking the right first steps, it may seem unattainable. However, it's possible that you already have everything you need to succeed in this industry; all you need to do is 1) find a market that meets the requirements of your particular criteria. 2) foster connections with a vast brokerage network and 3) eventually expand your portfolio through off-market transactions.

From the perspective of finding properties, the following fantastic websites are worth visiting:

- Property data - to learn the prices at which comparable homes are marketed and let in particular areas;
- The Land Registry, which describes the property's kind, number of bedrooms, etc.;
- The EPC register provides information about a property's square footage, condition, and cost-effectiveness as a place to live;
- For properties sold via auction, you can investigate properties on their websites before the auction takes place.

The best advice we can give you is to focus on one or two specific areas and become an expert in those subjects when it comes to finding real estate. Then, after some time, you'll discover you have the contacts and knowledge necessary to seize those opportunities.

"Property is a phenomenally lucrative and astoundingly simple investment vehicle, especially when you can purchase using almost entirely someone else's money!"
- Dolf De Roos

Market

Open-market VS Off-market

The open market is exposed to competition from unlimited prospective purchasers. Estate Agents work for the vendor to find the BEST buyer in the BEST position at the BEST price. Depending on the market conditions at any given time, the wave of enthusiasm from prospective purchasers will steer the eventual purchase price in favour of the vendor, which of course, is good for the vendor but not necessarily favourable to the Investor whose investment strategy is likely to be very much price sensitive. Remember, 'money is made on the purchase, not the sale'.

The open market can leave little opportunity as deals can be agreed upon relatively quickly, meaning that unless Investors are notified early on of upcoming properties, those investment opportunities are often missed altogether, with not even a chance to view, never mind, offer.

You may be wondering then why any Seller would even consider keeping their property off market when clearly, the chances of attracting a prospective purchaser at the best price seem significantly higher when it is placed 'on the market' and advertised through all of the portals. Benefits such as the following are clear examples;

- Providing a full set of property details will boost buyer confidence
- The Seller will gain access to a larger pool of prospective purchasers
- From that, they would perhaps be able to obtain

potentially better offers as more buyers compete against each other for theirs to be accepted

Of course, there are several disadvantages to selling on the open market, especially if there is a Tenant in situ:

- Additional selling expenses, such as Estate Agent fees
- It's less private and so more likely that neighbours will know that the property is for sale
- Suppose the property is Tenanted and sold to a purchaser wanting to move in after the completion of the sale. In that case, the Seller will clearly need to serve the relevant notice to the Tenant for them to vacate, as vacant possession will be required before the Conveyancers will allow contract completion to occur. (Over the years, I've seen many examples of situations where that process has taken longer due to a Tenant not being able to or not willing to vacate for whatever reason, which has then frustrated the sale and jeopardised the process)
- The tenants may feel that the sales process is more invasive and, therefore, less inclined to allow access for viewings to potential buyers

Going back to the point above regarding serving notice on the Tenant, you may wonder why there would be any complication if a Tenant is legally required to vacate after receiving that notice (s21 Form 1a). To expand on that full process, the serving of the s21 notice is only the first stage, which gives two months' notice of a Landlord's intention to regain full possession. During that time, the Tenant will be required to source alternative accommodation so that they can deliver that vacant possession back to the Landlord. All is well and good when a suitable property to move to is available in the first place. However, suppose availability is low or financially, they are unable to do so, and perhaps the Tenant intends to rely on the Local Authority to be rehoused. In that case, the process will become more drawn out. So, at the point of expiry of the s21 Notice, the Landlord will now be required to apply for an Accelerated Eviction notice from the County Court. There will be costs involved here that must be borne by the Landlord (at least initially). The Court will then serve that notice to the Tenant (assuming that the Tenant has not filed a defence to that Notice (and I will explain more about this with the dangers of getting this part wrong in the next chapter). Once that notice has expired (at which point you probably think that the Tenant should have vacated), if they have still been unsuccessful in finding alternative accommodation or are unwilling to do so, the third and final stage will be for the Landlord to request a Bailiff. There will be a further cost for this which again will need to be covered by the Landlord, and so, in summary, the whole process from start to finish can be extremely lengthy and costly. Add to that the problem that if a Tenant does vacate and the sale process is still ongoing in the meantime and perhaps worse still falls through in that time, then the Landlord is left with a property that is now vacant with no rent coming in and no buyer! So financially and logistically, this can be quite a painful process for the Seller! Through the Sourcing Service that we offer our Investor clients, a large proportion of our 'off market' opportunities come via our portfolio of Landlords we manage properties for, who then inform us of their intention to sell from time to time for whatever reason. The potential problems highlighted above make selling 'off market' appear to be the much more favoured approach and so effectively a win-win for both the Seller and Investor purchaser. The Seller gets to dispose of a property without any of the potential headaches coming into play and, better still, rental income right up to completion as the Tenant has not had to vacate and the Investor buyer gets to purchase in a closed environment without any of the usual competition from rival buyers. The Investor is given the opportunity directly and informed of the sale price the vendor wants to achieve. All due diligence is carried out by the Sourcing Agent in advance so that the Investor can decide quickly whether to purchase. Once the purchase price is agreed upon, the Investor has the opportunity to view and is free to opt-out if they later decide to for whatever reason.

In summary, let's examine the clear advantages of purchasing 'off market' against 'on market.'

- A firm asking price is obtained from the Sourcing Agent, which is then communicated to you together will all due diligence being performed so that you understand clearly the geared ROI from that opportunity
- A high chance that the property will be Tenanted, and so therefore, you'll have rent coming in from day one after the completion of the sale
- There is no Sourcing Fee to pay until the completion of the sale
- As the Sourcing Agent is taking care of the whole process, from locating properties to the due diligence, you, the Investor client, are free to go about your daily routine. You're then required to decide as to whether to purchase once a suitable property has been sourced

Regarding our own Property Sourcing service, the 'Buy To Let Advisory' that I mentioned earlier will have provided us with all of the information required to source the most suitable properties that match your identified investment strategy.

The primary aim is to secure a purchase of the ideal property that, on the open market, you may not have had the opportunity to purchase, what with competition from numerous buyers. The closed environment gives you that protection. The secondary aim is to secure a purchase below open market value.

It is important to note that purchasing under market value is not guaranteed and not the primary aim here but merely an added bonus if achieved.

"One of the best places to buy property is "Las Vegas" Due to being Desert Locked."
- Dolf De Roos

Money

I want to invest in real estate. But how much money do I need? Now, this is a question I'm regularly asked by my clients when interested in starting their journey in real estate investment. This particular section will delve into this area in great detail as it is significant in forming the basis of everything you'll do. So, you may wonder how seasoned Investors who've acquired numerous properties and built a successful portfolio actually managed to get that lump sum together to make their first purchase. Well, sometimes it will have come from a big break, such as finding that absolute bargain like a distressed sale where a Seller needs to offload a property in a hurry for which there may have been several reasons, such as rising debt or a marital split for example (remember the principle; 'money is made on the purchase, not on the sale'). But, on the other hand, if you manage to acquire a property significantly under market value, then immediately what you have at your disposal is collateral in the form of equity (the difference in current market value to the purchase price) which, of course, can then be borrowed against to re-invest whether that be into the same property to add to its value or to acquire additional properties. So, what if you don't even have the funds together to purchase that bargain property? Or let's even consider that you're unsuccessful in finding that instant money maker, and, being completely honest, such opportunities are few and far between in any case. Despite the general perception that you need a lot of money to make your first purchase, in reality, you could start your investment journey using completely someone else's.

So how can you invest in real estate with little to no cash? Well, there are a few tactics that you may want to consider where you won't even require much of your own money at all.

Rent to Rent is one of those, which means that you'll rent a property from a Landlord with the understanding that you will then sub-let to someone else at a higher level to make a profit over time. Naturally, the idea here is to find a Landlord who is happier with a lower-than-market level of rent in return for you having an Agreement in place (which should be a Management Agreement rather than a Tenancy Agreement) to pay consistently month in and month out regardless of whether you have the property let to an actual Tenant. Properties as prime candidates would be those where a Landlord may have struggled to let for whatever reason (however, it is, of course, worth bearing in mind that if the problems with letting are centred on the property rather than the property owner's ability, then it's also likely to be difficult for you to then let and so naturally, you should exercise caution before proceeding).

It could be let out as an HMO, serviced accommodation or any variety of different tactics. Since the Landlord's principle concern is a consistent monthly income, they may accept this even though they might earn more money by letting it out directly, as they perhaps don't want the inconvenience.

Although you'll be required to put a bit more effort into this type of setup, it can work quite effectively and as such, many people use this tactic as a launching pad to 'dip a toe into the ocean'. Another tactic to consider is a "purchase lease option".

This is quite comparable to rent to rent; the key distinction, however, is that if you choose, you also have the option to purchase the property in the future. For example, you agree on a purchase price today and then let it out in the meantime. Making money in the interim allows you to purchase in the future at the price you agreed upon years ago.

So even if you agree to purchase for the current full market value, that actual purchase price may have decreased in the future compared to what the property may technically be worth in time. Think of it as a double boost on the effects of inflation. The sum of money you agree on as a purchase price today will technically (due to inflation) be worth less in the future, aside from the fact that the property may have increased in value. Ultimately, you're still parting with the same amount of money that is now worth less! For this reason, it can be a pretty effective tactic.

Leveraging

Leveraging is a great way to get your money to work harder and more efficiently for you when investing in property. Property leveraging refers to buying a property with borrowed funds, typically from a lender, as opposed to paying for it totally out of one's own funds. The investor will contribute some of the entire purchase price with capital, leaving a certain amount of the purchase price as leverage. One of the reasons why buy-to-let real estate is such a desirable investment class is the availability of borrowing money to finance the purchase. Investors can distribute their wealth across several properties or buy a buy-to-let that costs more than their available funds, depending on their preference.

An investor must seek funding from a lender, such as a bank or building society, in order to leverage a property. In order to determine whether they are willing to lend money, the amount of the purchase price they will cover, and the terms on which they will do it, a lender will take into account the value of the property, the predicted rental income that it is expected to produce, as well as an investor's personal financial situation. For example, the lender might offer to lend 75% of the total purchase price, which would require the investor to provide 25% of their funds. For example, if a property costs £100,000, the lender will finance £75,000, and the investor will contribute £25,000 to the acquisition.

Leveraging in real estate investment can boost returns on capital because the borrower (investor) will gain from capital appreciation on the entire value increase of the property, not just on the capital they invested in it. An investor can use their available funds by using leverage and spreading that capital further than if they paid for the property in full by putting 25% down and utilising a mortgage with a 75% loan-to-value for the remainder of the purchase price. As a result, that same amount of capital can then generate x times as much of a return on investment as it would otherwise. The capital, not the loan amount, is relevant to the uplift. By only making well-informed investment decisions that have been planned and all factors are taken into account, such as mortgage repayments, the rental market, void periods, and the economic forecast, you can avoid hazards while using leverage.

When your current properties can help with the purchase of more buy-to-let properties, investment in real estate becomes more fascinating and has a higher potential payout. Leveraging real estate is a viable option for expanding your portfolio and purchasing more properties. For instance, an investor might begin by making a £30,000 down payment on each of the two properties and employing 70% leverage on each to purchase them for £100,000 each. I would anticipate that an investment made carefully in a hotspot for investments would increase in value by 20% over the course of five years, meaning that the two properties collectively have an additional £40,000 in equity. Remortgaging and removing roughly £30,000 from this equity pool will allow the investor to spend £100,000 on a third property, increasing their income and capital growth potential without adding significant cash to their portfolio.

Leverage is one of the best tools accessible to investors to increase the profit they may earn, especially through capital development. An investor can earn almost four times as much capital gain by leveraging their acquisition, depending on the loan-to-value. An investor must purchase real estate in areas with real potential for capital growth that offers high rental yields in a reliable market to achieve maximum success when using debt to fund a buy-to-let property.

Unlike investing in shares where your ROI is based on the value of the amount of shares you purchase, by leveraging a sum of money over more than one property (by taking out a mortgage for the larger percentage of the property), you benefit from the capital appreciation of the total value of the property rather than just the percentage of the purchase price you have paid cash for.

You're then earning capital appreciation and rental yield over multiple properties at the same time rather than just one where you have invested your own money into 100% of the purchase price

What type of mortgage is most suitable for you?
(i.e. Repayment or interest only)

The most common choice is interest only, as this greatly reduces the monthly payments, thus freeing up more of the rental income into your own pocket. However, in this scenario, you will not be reducing the balance of the mortgage, so you will need to consider your long-term intentions as you reach the end of the loan period, which is most commonly around 25 years. Then, your options will be either to repay the total cost of the loan (either from saved funds or by selling the property) or to re-mortgage for a further term.

So, whilst a repayment mortgage will mean higher monthly payments and, therefore, less monthly profit, you'll automatically own the property outright by the end of the mortgage term.

Whether to purchase in an individual's name or as a Ltd company?

Ltd company purchases are becoming a more popular choice to limit the amount of one's tax liability; however, you must also bear in mind that Interest rates on Ltd company purchases are not as competitive and, therefore, considerably higher. Consequently, I strongly advise you to speak with a reputable Accountant for further advice before making any such decisions.

Having an Independent Mortgage Broker is essential if you want a wide choice of Lenders at your disposal. All too often, I see situations where Investors make decisions on their choice of Lender from a significantly reduced list of options, purely down to the network the Mortgage Broker is part of. If you're only seeing a small selection of Lenders to choose from, then your best outcome will only be based on the best of those products, which won't necessarily be a true representation of what you could have had. Then, of course, the ability, expertise and knowledge of the products they offer will be what separates one Mortgage Broker from another. So, for this reason, your decision of which Broker to work with must be carefully considered. If your Broker isn't clued up with what they're doing and isn't able to guide and advise you towards the most suited mortgage products for you, then you could find yourself being more exposed to costly errors. Now you might ask yourself, 'if they're a Mortgage Broker by trade, then they know what they're doing, so what would be the difference from one to another if, generally, they all have more or less the same products? Well, I like to use the analogy of a car mechanic. From one car garage to the next, they all have mechanics who all supposedly know what they're doing; otherwise, they wouldn't be car mechanics in the first place, right? Well, how many times have you experienced a situation where one garage has perhaps not been able to identify the problem with the car and so not rectified it, perhaps used the wrong or cheap parts or worse still, made the situation worse!? Although this might seem like a far-out comparison, if you really think about it, this is exactly what is happening in the mortgage market because everyone's circumstances are different when it comes to applying for a particular product. It's not a 'one size fits all' situation. A highly experienced Mortgage Broker will know their products, the criteria set of those products and which fits best with you whilst being able to outline all of the pros and cons of each. I've seen many instances of the wrong product being selected, which has then wasted time and money for the Investor, where perhaps a more experienced and knowledgeable Broker would have known their products better, thus avoiding a pointless application if there was little to no chance of it going anywhere. A quick google search on statistics for the average fall-through rates in the UK will highlight one of the most common reasons as being mortgage-related. This then highlights the complexity of mortgage applications. Therefore it needs to be one of the most carefully planned if your Investment strategy is going to stand any chance of being successful.

If your strategy is based on achieving a higher capital appreciation, the aim is to build up equity growth over time that can then be leveraged against to be released as a deposit towards further property purchases

Another way of building up a sum of money is in the BRRRR model (Buy, refurb, rent, remortgage, repeat). This involves purchasing property in a dilapidated state, thus purchasing considerably under market value compared to a similar property in a 'done up' condition, refurbishing and then letting out at the highest market value rent and then re-mortgaging against the new increased sales value of property to release equity for the next purchase under the same strategy.

"Buy land. They're not making it anymore."
- Mark Twain

The Stress-Free M.P Predictor Framework™

"It's not whether you're right or wrong but how much
money you make when you're right and how much you lose
when you're wrong."
~ George Soros

Increases

Due to the recent cost-of-living problem and inflation
hitting a new 40-year high (at the time of writing), the UK
financial system has hit a challenging time. In addition, in
their attempts to curb that level of inflation, the Bank of
England, through their Monitory Policy Committee (MPC)
meetings, are forced to increase the base rate of interest rates.

Just when the UK believed it had successfully survived
COVID-19 and the worst of Brexit, little did we realise that
there was still more uncertainty to come. However, property
experts remain optimistic about their industry even when
faced with such challenges.

The cost of living had increased due to COVID, Brexit,
and Russia's invasion of Ukraine, which raised inflation to
9.4%.

In response, the Bank of England continually raised
interest rates. We witnessed how much the economy can
suffer through legislative leadership changes, which would
only add to that uncertainty.

The outlook for the economy has been dim in the light of
all that uncertainty, but the property mortgage market has
looked slightly better.

In this section, I will cover 'Knowing how to predict and ride the waves of uncertainty and maximise your return on investment' using my 'Stress-Free M.P. Predictor framework™'. M.P. Predicator indicates the 'Market' and 'Prices' within the industry. I will cover the two main returns on investment, i.e. Capital appreciation and yield. With this understanding, you will be able to use that to maximise the gains (based on your chosen investment strategy) when the market is good and minimise the losses when the market is bad. So, this involves you putting in the research to ensure that you are making informed decisions on what to buy.

"Some people look for a beautiful place. Others make a place beautiful."
- Hazrat Inayat Khan

Market

What is the impact of uncertainty on the market?

Market uncertainty occurs when there is high market volatility, and investors find it challenging to predict the present and future market circumstances.

Financial markets: Investors demand a better rate of return on their capital under uncertain circumstances by paying higher risk premiums. This implies that at periods when the central bank may lower its policy rate, which is typically done when the economy slows down, the cost of lending may rise.

The idea of buy-to-let is not new; it is a term familiar to most people and has long been a favourite among investors. Buy-to-let mortgages account for about 12% of all mortgages in the UK, making them an important component of the real estate industry. But how do you truly profit from buying and letting out properties, and what factors should prospective investors take into account before entering the market?

The fact that people can profit from buy-to-let investments in two separate ways—through rental yields and capital growth—is one of the factors contributing to their popularity. It's vital to understand both of these if you want to invest. Still, it's also important to have an opinion on which is most important to you because this will eventually determine the type and location of the property you invest in. Even if you are an experienced Landlord with expertise in the field, the precise definitions of these terms can still be a little confusing. In order to help, I have compiled a list of essential advice covering the two most crucial phases of the lettings process. I also examine the possibility of prioritising one over the other for better results.

If you're considering becoming a Landlord, you've probably heard the terms "rental yields" and "capital gain/appreciation" used frequently. But what do these terms actually mean?

Understanding rental yields

Rental yield is essentially the amount of rent you may anticipate receiving from your property over the course of a year relative to the cost you spent for it. As long as you continue letting out your property, this yearly return can continue for a very long time. Therefore, the return on investment is better the higher the yield. When determining the rental yield, you must take into account a number of factors, including the purchase price or current worth of the property and the anticipated annual rent.

Once clear on these factors, you may use the following formula to determine your home's prospective rental yield. You divide the annual rent of a property by its purchase price and then multiply by 100.

Here is one instance. If you purchase a property for £400,000 and earn £15,000 a year in rental revenue, your yield would be 3.75%. (£15,000 ÷ £400,000 x 100).

The yield would be greater at 4.8% if the property had a purchase price of £250,000 and you earned £12,000 per year in rental income.

According to this estimate, you typically find greater rental yields in areas with lower property prices but still with competitive rentals. Even though rental income is typically lower on more affordable properties, larger yields are typically produced. That's because there is a smaller initial investment and hence less pressure on yields.

Naturally, your return on investment will be better if the property can reach a higher yield. Therefore, anticipated rental yields are a smart approach for buy-to-let Landlords to determine whether or not a specific property is a wise investment. Also, Landlords must know the distinction between gross yield and net yield. The computation above provides you with the gross yield; however, to calculate your net yield (i.e., the amount of money you really take home), you must then deduct all the costs related to letting out a property from your annual rental amount.

These costs include letting agent fees, maintenance and repair charges, and Landlord insurance.

Understanding capital appreciation

The money you earn due to the rise in the value of your property over time is known as capital appreciation or capital gain. This factor is relevant if and when you sell the asset. Even though this is more of a long-term aspect, it has gained importance during the past few years due to the country's skyrocketing real estate values, which have quickly made many investors wealthy.

In reality, the value of the £7.6 trillion British real estate market keeps breaking records. Over the previous 20 years, it has outperformed the FTSE All Share Index, cash, and gold, with property prices doubling on average every 10 to 15 years.

Which one ought to be your primary focus?

Both sorts of returns are significant to everyone because they are beneficial to the majority of buy-to-let investors. However, where and what you buy depends on the kind of return you decide to concentrate on when setting out your strategy.

People who concentrate on rental yields frequently want to increase their regular income in the short term and may consider the investment a second pension. On the other hand, those that place a strong emphasis on capital growth are long-term investors who may be planning how they will support their children, fund their retirement, or just protect their money against low returns.

Choosing a property type depending on the return

Your investment objectives and interest in either of these two returns will determine where and what to buy.

London offers excellent returns on capital appreciation, but the cost of housing is expensive, and the rental yield is relatively low. This has been made worse by the pandemic, which, according to Hamptons, has resulted in a 17.7% decline in rental yields in February 2021 compared to the same month the year before, despite relatively unchanged home prices. According to a study from The FT, the typical London rental return actually decreased to 3.8% in December 2020.

The opposite is true for rural areas and typically northern locations with lower property prices. According to InventoryBase, Glasgow (7.52%) is the best city for rental yields. In September 2022, the property portal Zoopla calculated the gross yield for Peterborough, where I am based, to be 5.49%. According to propertydata.co.uk, in 2022, the average gross yield for the U.K. was 3.63%.

Commuter towns, particularly those on the outskirts of London, which typically have high statistics and where properties are more inexpensive, but renter demand is high, are another excellent option for rental yields.

In 83% of local authorities last year, flats produced greater average gross returns than any sort of housing, according to Hamptons, who also claim that apartments give higher yields than houses.

It's critical for anyone considering lower-yield investments to keep in mind that it will become more challenging to obtain buy-to-let mortgages, which base their interest rate on rental yield rather than always considering the borrower's credit score.

As previously mentioned, London remains a top choice for people seeking excellent capital appreciation, as are other densely populated cities all throughout the nation. Consider London's capital gain as an example: Twenty years ago, hypothetically speaking, a £100 investment in the London real estate market would be worth £1,290 today. Gold would cost £355 and cash savings £266, whereas the same amount put in the FTSE All Share index would be £525.

Investors should keep an eye out for places that are regenerating outside of those locations. There are areas of renewal all around the country where property prices are rising quickly from a low foundation, and investors can expect excellent long-term profits. For example, 'Seven Capital' claims that recent years have seen significant revitalization in Birmingham, Leeds, and Derby.

Having trouble deciding what you prefer? The likes of Manchester and Liverpool are experiencing good capital growth as well as rental income if you're on the fence and want to try and go for both returns.

Despite recent changes to tax laws that may have had an adverse effect on investors, buy-to-let investing ultimately continues to be a desirable asset class. Because of the ongoing relatively low-interest rates, buy-to-let returns continue to outperform other types of investments, particularly cash held in a savings account. Buy-To-Let Interest rates have increased recently from around 2% to 4.7%. Understanding your objectives concerning capital growth and rental yield is the key to success; doing so will ultimately help you determine whether or not to invest.

What Is the Difference Between Return and Yield?

The profitability of an investment over a specific time period, sometimes annually, can be calculated using both yields and return. In contrast to the return, normally reported as a cash number, the yield is the income an investment generates over time and is frequently expressed as a percentage.

The return is backwards-looking, while the yield is forward-looking.

Yield

Yield is the income obtained in return for an investment, like the interest from keeping securities. Based on the investment's cost, current market value, or face value, the yield is often represented as an annual percentage rate. The yield may be seen as known or anticipated depending on the security, which may suffer value fluctuations.

Yield has a prospective nature. Additionally, it excludes capital gains from its calculations and only counts the income an investment earns, such as interest and dividends (or rent in this case). This income is calculated throughout a certain period and then annualised under the presumption that interest, dividends or rent payments would continue to be made at the same pace.

Return

Return, often known as the financial gain or loss on an investment, is frequently expressed as the change in an investment's cash value over time. On the other hand, return, often known as total return, describes how much money an investor makes from an investment during a specific time period. Rental income (yield) and capital gains (such as increased property prices) are all included in the total return. A return is, therefore, retroactive or backwards-looking. More specifically, a Geared Return on Investment is a clearer way of looking at the return on property investment as it takes into account the rental yield, combined with the capital appreciation, fewer outgoings such as maintenance etc., against the actual amount of money invested into the property (the deposit, rather than the full purchase price).

Risk and Yield

The yield received on investment includes risk as a significant component. Therefore, the potential yield is larger when the risk is greater.

The Rate of Return vs Yield

Both rates of return and yield reflect how investments performed over a predetermined time period (usually one year), although they have small and occasionally significant differences. A specific technique to express the total return on an investment that indicates the percentage increase over the initial investment cost is by using the rate of return. (Yield does not factor in capital gains when calculating the amount of income that has been returned on an investment based on starting cost).

The formula for the rate of return is:
Total rental income plus the total amount of capital appreciation, fewer outgoings (including mortgage payment and maintenance), against the original amount of funds put down (deposit).

Capital

What Is Capital Appreciation?

An increase in an investment's market value is known as capital appreciation. The difference between an investment's acquisition and sale prices is known as capital appreciation. For instance, if a property is purchased for £200,000 and the price increases to £250,000, the investor will have made £50,000 in capital gains. The £50,000 gained converts to a capital gain when the investor sells the stock.

Understanding Capital Appreciation

The portion of an investment where market price increases exceed the investment's original purchase price or cost basis is referred to as capital appreciation. In various markets and asset classes, capital appreciation can happen for a variety of different causes. For example, investments in financial assets for capital growth include the following: Real estate holdings, mutual funds, or funds with a pool of money invested in different assets, as well as exchange-traded funds (ETFs) and securities that track indices like the S&P 500, are all examples of holdings; Commodities like copper or oil as well as Stocks or other equities.

"Games are won by players who focus on the playing field—not by those whose eyes are glued to the scoreboard. If you instead focus on the prospective price change of a contemplated purchase, you are speculating. There is nothing improper about that. I know, however, that I am unable to speculate successfully, and I am skeptical of those who claim sustained success at doing so."

- Warren Buffet

Prices

How will the housing market be affected by rising interest rates?

Without first examining inflation, it is impossible to discuss rising interest rates.

The Office of National Statistics determines the cost of a basket of goods by looking at 18,000 prices for approximately 700 products to determine the rate of inflation. At the time of writing, the inflation rate was at 9.4%, the highest level since 1990.

The Central Bank of England released significant additional funds that the government had borrowed for the NHS, furlough programmes, bounce bank loans, and the pandemic. The economy received that borrowed money, but as more money then circulates, the value decreases.

The majority of people will have already felt the impact of inflation as well as that of the pandemic on the supply chain as the price of food and raw materials has increased. In addition, rent has increased by as much as 20% in some regions, energy costs are rising swiftly, and fuel prices have increased.

Due to modifications to the basket of products in recent years, many experts think the cost of living has increased significantly more than the 8.6% figure stated. Inflation can be advantageous for investors or people who depend on the housing market slowing down, but for many people, it will mean less disposable income.

The interest rate determines the cost of borrowing money and using a bank to store your funds. This is because the amount you borrow or save over the course of the year is used to determine interest rates. As a result, if you deposited £1,000 and earned 1% interest, you would have £1,010 a year later.

Why Might Inflation Benefit Property Investors?

For the appropriate people, the effects of inflation on the housing market might be advantageous. If we as people are in debt, inflation may manifest itself in the most beneficial way possible. When investing in real estate, you borrow money to pay for the purchase.

For real estate investors, financing the investment in the property typically involves borrowing money. Typically, purchasers receive a 75% loan-to-value mortgage and may provide a 25% down payment, i.e. £200,000 property will have a £50,000 deposit. If we had an interest-only mortgage over time, we would pay the interest each month yet have a remaining £150,000 balance. If we have a 20-year mortgage, we will still owe £150,000 at the end of that term; however, as inflation increases, the real value of the mortgage decreases. Therefore, the purchasing power of £150,000 decreases as inflation increases.

The property you purchased for £200,000 may cost £600,000, let's say, in 20 years, but your mortgage will still only be £150,000. If you sell that property in 20 years, you will be required to pay capital gains taxes (unless it's your own home), but even after paying the tax, you will still have enough money to clear the mortgage and still have extra money left over. If you own several properties, the proceeds from the sale of one property can be used to pay off the mortgages on the others as you try to amass a portfolio free of debt. As a result, inflation makes investing in real estate financially feasible. Higher interest rates are one danger, but this can be avoided with a fixed-term mortgage.

What should I buy, where, and how should I buy?

As letting agents, we are on hand to guide and advise you on suitable properties to purchase as an investment based on your investment strategy. However, as Landlords, you need to make sure you conduct your own research and ensure you understand precisely what you are after.

Remember:
- Purchase at the right Price
- Look for something that Rents Well
- With a good return

"Money is made on the Purchase, not on the Sale!"

What should you be on the lookout for when buying real estate? Although location is always important, many other aspects can influence whether an investment is good for you. Here are a few crucial factors to consider if you intend to engage in the real estate market.

1. Property Location

Why It Matters

The phrase "location, location, location" is still true and is one of the most crucial elements in real estate investing success. Residential property assessments heavily consider the status of the community, green space, beautiful landscapes, and proximity to amenities. In addition, when valuing real estate, accessibility to markets, warehouses, transportation hubs, and motorways is crucial.

What to Check Out

The medium- to long-term outlook for how the neighbourhood is anticipated to change over the investment period is crucial when determining where to purchase a property. For instance, the quiet open space behind a property might one day be transformed into a busy manufacturing plant, lowering its value. Examine the ownership and intended use of the immediate locations where you propose to make your investment in great detail.

Getting in touch with the town hall or other government organisations in charge of zoning and urban planning is one approach to learning more about the prospects for the area around the property you are contemplating. You can then decide whether the long-term planning in the region is advantageous or unfavourable to your own strategy for the property.

2. An assessment of the property

Why It Matters

Real estate valuation is crucial for financing the purchase and listing price, investment research, insurance, and taxation—all of which rely on it.

What to Check Out

Typical techniques for valuing real estate include:

- Approach to sales comparison: recent comparable sales of properties with comparable features—the most typical and appropriate for both new and old properties.
- Cost-effective for new construction is the cost of the land and the building less depreciation.

- Rent-friendly income strategy based on anticipated cash inflows

3. Investment Objectives and Horizon

Why It Matters

Lack of clarity regarding the aim may result in unanticipated outcomes, including financial distress—especially if the investment is mortgaged—given real estate's low liquidity and high value.

4. Anticipated cash flows and potential for profit

Why It Matters

Cash flow is the amount of money that remains after expenses. Positive cash flow is crucial to a strong rate of return on an investment property.

What to Check Out

Create predictions for the upcoming profit and expense modes:

- Expected rental income cash flow (inflation favours Landlords for rental income)
- Expected rise in intrinsic value as a result of sustained price growth.
- Gains from depreciation (and available tax benefits)
- Analysis of the costs and benefits of refurbishing before selling to acquire a higher price
- Mortgaged loans' costs and benefits are compared to value growth.

You can invest in real estate in a variety of ways and reap the perks that go along with it. For example, some investors decide to buy older properties with the goal of renovating and reselling them. Despite the lengthy nature of the undertaking, this strategy can be extremely profitable.

An alternate way to invest is by purchasing new construction off-plan. This method of investing is buying real estate before it is finished and then letting it out for high yields and capital profits.

We advise beginning with one of the aforementioned strategies to prevent stress, confusion, and the inability to generate revenue. As a beginner investor, combining different strategies can jeopardise your success.

What kinds of investments are there in real estate?

Before starting your real estate enterprise, the distinctions between each investment kind and how you might profit from them should be noted and understood. Once you have decided on your investment focus, you need to conduct extensive research on how the market for real estate operates and how to make profitable investments. Developing an appropriate plan before investing in an investment property is essential to ensure you have the necessary resources and knowledge.

Traditional investment property for buy-to-let

Buy-to-let residential properties, the most common investment type, produce returns from rental income because they are bought with the goal of letting them out to tenants. Due to the lesser financial output required and the normally lower costs involved with owning a buy-to-let home, this investment type is generally regarded as having minimal risk. The investor can earn from a steady rental income sufficient to cover monthly mortgage payments and maintenance charges while leaving room for profit. A buy-to-let investment is ideal for individuals wishing to grow a portfolio and receive long-term financial benefits. Landlords can also profit from capital growth returns when the property is eventually sold.

HMOs

The market for houses with multiple occupants (HMOs) is becoming increasingly lucrative for Landlords looking to maximise their profits and gain from higher yields. HMO consists mostly of multiple bedrooms and communal spaces like kitchens and bathrooms. Landlords prefer larger buildings with several tenants residing there thanks to the multiple sources of revenue that may be collected simultaneously. In addition, Landlords experience little income loss from void periods when multiple tenants are assigned to a single property since other tenants can fill the voids. However, HMOs have disadvantages in that intricate licencing regulations can be in place depending on the region the property is located in. Additionally, purchasing an HMO entails effective property management, upkeep, and extra expenses.

Student-rental homes

Student housing generates income from rental fees in a manner that is fairly similar to that of conventional residential rental property. The tenant kinds and suggested sites, as student housing should always be within close proximity to educational institutions in the UK's top cities, are the key variations between the two types of buy-to-let properties. Due to the low initial investment costs and high average profits, this sort of real estate investment is a suitable place for beginners to start. As the UK's higher education reputation continues to be unmatched and draws thousands of students worldwide each year, the demand for student housing in the country is on the rise.

What to look for in a rental property for investment

Your target audience is a fantastic place to start when looking at the finest areas and property kinds to invest in. When choosing a property, you'll be well prepared if you understand the ideal tenant type, their lifestyles, possible revenue, and property needs. Starting with modest apartments, HMOs, or student housing may be the most appropriate approach to guarantee that your investment makes a return, depending on your financial circumstances and available finances. On the other hand, you may want to think about property development if you have a large amount of money to invest.

Your quest for attractive investment options should centre on location. Therefore, you should research prime locations that will appeal to tenants and investors, taking into account the strength and anticipated expansion of the following factors.

Property costs - The average property costs in the area where you want to invest should be within your means. Similar to average home prices, which reflect the expenses individuals are ready to pay and the incomes of the local population, average property prices are a useful indicator of the performance of the local real estate market.

Average rents - In general, average rent costs fluctuate according to a city's economic development, how close a property is to the city centre, and the demand for real estate in that area. Tenants in many of the fast-growing cities in the UK are significantly more likely to pay higher rent. However, low average rental rates guarantee steady and long-term tenant demand.

Population - Using the expected population growths for each town and city that you are interested in, you should be able to identify popular locations.

Degree of demand - To underline the preceding point, any buy-to-let, HMO, or build-to-rent must have a high level of rental demand. Your property should sustain a high level of demand if you choose a location with easy access to transportation, close proximity to educational institutions, and lucrative employment prospects.

Career options - Many UK towns have developed into well-known business hubs for a number of the biggest industries and commercial sectors in the country. You greatly increase the likelihood that your property won't ever remain empty by giving the community a piece of real estate in a place with plenty of employment prospects.

Potential for capital growth: Investment-grade locations offer a promising potential for the price increase, with predictions for an exponential rise in property prices in the years to come.

Type of asset

The facilities, style, and size of a property will also impact the type of tenant it draws, even though your budget and financial position will play a large role in determining the property type. A roomy, suburban home with a huge garden is more likely to appeal to a family with children than, say, a modern, small apartment, which is more likely to draw young professionals and couples. An expensive down payment and ongoing maintenance are possible when buying a property. These assets also typically generate the largest revenues. Family homes and premium city centre property developments are good investments if your primary goals are high yields and substantial rental income.

Physical state of the property

The state of your investment property is important for determining future maintenance needs and potential costs. For example, properties with high-quality and long-lasting furnishings have higher occupancy and lower turnover rates and require less upkeep. According to reports, most seasoned investors only spend 3% of their annual income on upkeep.

Additionally, buying a property in an off-plan development is a great investment since skilled builders ensure that new construction adheres to building codes and features high-end designs.

What are the possible hazards of investing in real estate for development?

Although one of the best ways to create passive income and cash flow is to invest money in real estate, there are many factors to consider before making an investment. For example, you should consider charges such as capital gains tax, rising interest rates, legal fees, and stamp duty, in addition to the level of risk associated with investing.

You can avoid any severe setbacks and financial burdens by preparing for the potential pitfalls listed below:

Market turbulence - The initial yield, which is computed by dividing the current yearly rent by the property's worth, is used to estimate a property's value. Any up-front expenses for purchases are included. The initial yield can therefore change from year to year. In general, the yield will unavoidably mirror the real estate market's economic cycle. You can develop a workable strategy for your real estate investment by setting reasonable expectations for your profits and any probable short-term volatility. Putting aside emergency savings to act as a financial buffer is another approach to ensure that market changes do not greatly impact you.

Rent arrears - When rent payments are past late, it might affect the Landlord's ability to make a living. Even though payment deadlines are specified in rental agreements, missed payments can still happen. If the amount of unpaid rent increases month after month, eviction and legal action may be warranted. You can use a variety of tactics to help tenants with their rent payments. However, I strongly advise that you have a suitable Insurance policy to protect you against such scenarios. In fact, as part of my Letting Agency's service to our Landlord clients (which I shall explain further in the following chapter), our top-level package guarantees rent payments consistently and punctually to them on the rent due date, month in and month out regardless of whether the tenant has actually met that commitment. Furthermore, it also covers the full procedure and associated costs of tenant eviction if required.

Property damage - It is important to remember that general wear and tear on the property will occur over time while it is inhabited and eventually become evident. It is crucial to consider the wall and flooring materials used to make the most of your asset and make it as lasting as possible. Additionally, after a tenancy expires, you should take the necessary actions to address stains, minor damage, and blemishes. Although Landlords can claim from deposits, they should exercise discretion and carefully consider the consequences before refusing to return the down payment (which I shall explain again in the next chapter).

What advantages do off-plan buildings offer?

Off-plan property developments are, quite simply, unfinished construction projects. Additional investment opportunities are developed as more and more construction plans are put forth in an effort to address the nation's housing shortfall. One of the most profitable investment strategies is purchasing off-the-plan real estate, which is swiftly gaining popularity among many investors.

Invest in a development project early on to maximise your long-term return on investment. The development of technology has made it possible for potential investors to study extensive design plans created by developers, giving them a thorough understanding of how the finished property would appear. Investors can decide whether or not the finished product will be a profitable asset in their portfolio by carefully reviewing the plans and blueprints.

Reduced prices

Off-plan properties have low prices associated with this investment option, which is one of its key draws. Early investment enables the purchaser to acquire a property for less than market value. By the time a construction project is finished, property values are typically anticipated to increase. On rare occasions, purchasing many properties from a developer with a wide range of upcoming developments might also lead to further savings.

Increase in value

If you choose to invest early in a future venture, the property's value can increase as it is being built. At the end of the day, this would give real estate investors immediate equity. Data shows that prices rise by an average of 4% annually in the UK, where property prices tend to climb swiftly. As capital growth is not assured, a medium- to a long-term investment strategy is nevertheless advised. Location has a significant impact on capital growth. A city's property price will increase if there is a high demand for housing, positive growth prospects, and impending investment.

As we have already demonstrated, investing in buy-to-let real estate may be very profitable and offer an incalculable number of advantages. For example, having many properties under your belt might result in significant long-term returns, while investing in a single property may result in profits and long-term capital growth.

It can be in your best interest to start small and add more properties as you go in order to establish a larger portfolio of buy-to-let properties. You will gain the knowledge and expertise you need from this to design your investment strategy and create a portfolio successfully.

Adding Value in the short term

So how can you beat the market in the SHORT TERM?

Warren Buffett says of investment strategies...Look to see what everyone else is doing and then

GO IN THE OPPOSITE DIRECTION!

If you're looking for a FAST return on the property, this may be via

- Repossessions
- Conversions to HMOs
- Local Housing Authority market
- Properties needing work or with specific problems

Also

Look at your investment type, experience and facilities available to you and consider how you can add value to a property. For example, if you buy a property and make improvements to it, then it WILL increase in value.

Suppose you are not a builder look for properties that have something missing or are perhaps lacking something. For example, could you add a garage, downstairs w.c, en-suite, new kitchen, shower, drive, new windows, central heating, or carry out redecoration? In addition, you want to look for something with a job that is too small for a builder but too big for a young couple. You may even want to consider adding an extension.

Repossessions

There are plenty of repossessions on the market, but many people want them, so how do you find them?

Searching Out Bargains

Look for: properties with -

- "no upward chain"
- 2 For Sale Boards
- A4 pieces of paper in the window
- Yellow tape over the water services in the internal photos on Rightmove
- "Public Notice" adds in the paper

Remember that the Estate Agent's job when selling a repossession is to get the highest price, so gazumping is commonplace here. As such, you must be ready to pay for your dream of profit as it's part of the bargain.

What type of Investor am I?

In summary, consider the following to understand

- Are you a high-risk or low-risk investor?
- Are you seeking capital appreciation or income?
- If capital, do you want it immediately or in the long term?
- If you are looking for Income, do you want high-income "active" or medium-income "passive"?
- What money do you have available now?
- Are you experienced in DIY, or do you have contact in the trade?
- Do you want to build a portfolio that will be self-funding?
- Do you currently own properties that you want to form part of your rental portfolio?

KEY TAKEAWAYS:

- An important factor to remember is that money is made on the PURCHASE, not the SALE
- There are two ways to look at your return on investment (Capital Appreciation which is the value increase of property over time, and yield, which is the return from the rental income against the money invested)
- To date, over the last 20 years, capital appreciation (average price increases) in the UK has run at 9% annually
- Where I am based (in Peterborough, UK) as a geared return on investment (based on a 25% deposit, with a 6.6% average capital appreciation over the last 20 x years, and average rental return combined) the average is 38%. That is a 38% annual geared return on your 25% deposit
- What we need to do is look at trends in terms of which areas are popular or in high demand for decent property. Where is sought after, and where are not many more properties being built?
- More importantly, what makes one area more sought after than another (high-performing school/s in the catchment area, good accessibility to and from, picturesque local views and scenery). These are the kinds of factors which are likely to affect the rate of capital appreciation.
- Over time, the level of property prices will both rise and fall, but putting in the research before your property purchase minimises the rate at which a reducing price market will affect your investment.
- Depending on the time span that you are looking to invest, ultimately, over a long enough period, your property investment will increase. So, the trick is knowing which type of property and where is most likely to gain the highest capital appreciation over

time. From that, you can then work back to where you want to focus your investment strategy, i.e. if you wish to aim for high capital appreciation or high yield (remember, you can't get high levels of both, so it's one or the other or a combination of the both but at lower levels on each, *refer to the capital cash flow calculator*)

- Adding value in the short term (buying property below market value based on its dilapidated state or perhaps adding features to the property to make it more attractive such as a garage, downstairs w.c, opening out a kitchen and dining room to make it a more practical and appealing kitchen/diner, adding an extension, converting a garage or loft, en-suite, new kitchen, a driveway, central heating, new windows (you want a job that is too small for a builder but too big for a young couple)
- Buying repossessions can be a good way of purchasing under market value, but you need to understand the process and risks in terms of competing buyers over the duration of your property purchase (higher offers coming in before completion of the sale)
- Consider whether the property could be converted to an HMO. HMOs will then create a higher income model, which could then make the property a more attractive model if you sell on (HMOs are massively growing in popularity with investors)
- Could the property even be used as a building plot (whether knocking the existing property down or keeping that in place and building additional property/ies within the land coverage)
- Could the property be developed into flats and then sold off or let out?

"Don't wait to buy real estate.
Buy real estate and wait."
- Will Rogers

THE ULTIMATE K.P.I. BENCHMARK FOR LETTING AGENTS ™

'Success is not measured by what you do compared to
what somebody else does. Success is measured by what you
do compared to what you are capable of doing.'
~Zig Ziglar

So you've started to build your BTL property portfolio,
mastering the sourcing of 'off-market' opportunities and
combining that with your outlined strategy to help ensure you
get the most out of your investment. Now all that remains is
to secure reliable tenants, and away you go. However, here's
the thing, unless you're managing that tenancy to the letter of
the law, any chance you had of the venture being successful
can quickly dwindle away in a painful and costly manner.

Over the years, I have seen far too many examples of
Landlords who have been naïve to the legislation within the
private rental sector, and I'm not even referring to those who
have no desire or consideration towards being compliant.
These are people who have every intention of providing safe,
habitable accommodation for their tenants and will be
responsive to any issues that may come along; however,
unfortunately for them, the letting of residential property is a
complex system full of more than 170 x pieces of legislation!
Yes, I too was shocked when I counted them up, and this is
why we must be absolutely certain that if we are going to
stand any chance of achieving what we set out to, then we

need to ensure we know what we're getting ourselves into. In a world where tenants are becoming ever more aware of their rights, combined with opportunism and people looking to benefit from others' mistakes or misfortune, the smallest error could prove detrimental on a massive scale. In some cases, we could be talking about a missing document that should have been provided to the tenant at a certain time. One single piece of paper that might not have seemed quite so important at the time, so much so that it wasn't even realised as required, never mind forgotten, and you now have a Tenancy with potential issues when it comes to enforcing the tenants' obligations or regaining possession of the property.

Several years ago, I remember a situation where a friend of mine who had decided to dabble in BTL investment got himself into a pickle with one of his tenancies. He had been managing the Tenancies himself, using my services only to find and qualify suitable tenants for him to then take over, dealing with Tenancy renewals and all other procedures along the way. Following his engagement to his partner, it was then his intention for them to move into one of his properties that he then had intended to make his principle residence and family home. He had attempted, rather complacently, to serve his tenants with notice for them to vacate, then left the property vacant for them to move into just before their planned date for the wedding. Just through conversation with him at that time, the realisation quickly set in that he had made more than one costly error and stood little to no chance of him being able to regain possession in any timely or effective manner. On that occasion, however, he was fortunate as we were then able to negotiate with the tenants leading to them consenting to early termination of tenancy on the grounds of their own financial hardship at that time, but the outcome could have been so different! He would have been in a situation where he'd have been required to re-serve notice, potentially adding at least a further 4-6 months onto the likely timescale, which no doubt will have then thrown his wedding plans into turmoil.

Tenancy Management is not to be taken lightly. What may appear to be a cost-saving exercise by 'going it alone' and cutting out the Agent could very easily result in a bigger financial headache, what with the risks of civil and criminal prosecution when getting it wrong! The amount of your own valuable time that is likely to be taken up by managing your tenancies, before we even consider the financial impact of errors or inefficiencies of that management, could result in a situation where you're quite literally 'stepping over pounds to save pennies'!

To help give you a clear understanding of the minimum capabilities that your chosen Letting Agency should be working to in order to be making the most effective use of your property investment whilst safeguarding you against Landlord liability, I've created a unique framework that will guide you in the right direction towards your desired goals, called 'The Ultimate K.P.I. benchmark for Letting Agents™.

- Know-how – the background procedures you should be aware of as a Landlord to ensure total compliance
- Preservation – ensuring effective systems are in place for efficient management and maintenance of the properties
- Inhabitant – the quality and suitability of your sourced and selected tenants

Being a Landlord can be extremely time-consuming and not to mention daunting when you consider your responsibilities combined with the consequences of getting it wrong! Using a competent and professional Letting Agency should enable you to concentrate on your own affairs so that you can use your time more wisely, as no doubt you'll have your own career to worry about, not to mention any efforts to expand your property portfolio gradually. Tenancy management in itself is a full-time profession and is certainly not something that can be 'dipped in and out of' from time to time. You need a 'finger on the pulse' at all times as quite literally anything can happen at any time and in an instant, so without a reliable system in place, things can go wrong very quickly.

Perhaps three of the most likely benefits of your Letting Agency's representation are their negotiating skills enabling them to secure you a Tenancy at the most achievable rental figure to the most suitable of tenants, a firm understanding of the procedures required to ensure strict compliance with the legislation and of course, the means to keep everything under control with regards to ongoing maintenance whilst also placing great focus on the relationship between Landlord and Tenant. Through this, they should be able to manage those situations to minimise disputes between both parties, thus saving you time, money and effort through a smooth and effective system. The above should not be taken lightly as, indeed, there will be Letting Agencies out there who, through their own efforts to secure your business, will focus their strategy on their price offering to attract you to them rather than the key principles that will have a bearing on the quality of their service to you and your tenants. Looking at this realistically, an Agency's ability to carry out effective Tenancy management will depend massively on their infrastructure and its continual development, which, remember, needs to focus on many key areas, such as compliance, to name but a few. In addition, they should be aware of the legislation affecting the private rental sector and the continual changes and amendments to it. So for these reasons, your choice of Letting Agency should not be focused on fee level alone and should certainly not be the determining factor.

Focusing on legislation for a moment, the Private Rental Sector has undergone numerous regulatory reforms, particularly since the pandemic, including the (temporary) ban on tenant evictions and so if the Lettings Industry is not your main profession, then staying current with these developments will feel like a constant battle and strain on your time. Fortunately, a qualified and knowledgeable Lettings Agency will be able to assist you with total compliance, thus helping to avoid fines for failing to fulfil your commitments without you having to put in your own research.

The Benefits of Using a Letting Agency

Using a Letting Agency makes sense for numerous reasons, some less apparent than others.

Time

I've lost count of the times I've spoken with private Landlords who have told me, "I have a Plumber and Electrician, so I don't require a Letting Agent as they'll go and sort any issues for me as and when". The truth is, attending to general maintenance is only a small fraction of the time it will take to fully perform your duties as a responsible Landlord. When you consider areas such as;

- the advertising techniques behind securing reliable tenants in a timely and effective manner,
- the thorough referencing process to sift out those less desirable,
- the paperwork exercise required (not just at the start of the Tenancy but throughout, especially with regard to required certification),
- the ongoing response to maintenance issues,
- the providing of a system enabling tenants to report urgent matters to you 24/7,
- the documenting of all tenancy matters (essential should there ever be a dispute with the tenant),
- the ongoing monitoring of rental payments and a system whereby such arrears are dealt with in compliance with Tenancy law,
- the procedure of dealing with Tenancy breaches,

including court action if required,

- the reliance on a strong 'check in' and 'check out' procedure to safeguard your use of the tenant's deposit should it be required,
- the process of deposit dispute settlement in the event that the tenant disagrees with the deposit settlement proposal,
- your ongoing monitoring of legislation developments,

and of course, all of this on top of your own profession, then it is clear that the responsibility of being a competent private Landlord is certainly a time-consuming one. A professional and reputable Lettings Agency should be able to take the whole strain away from you, leaving you free to reap the rewards with zero involvement.

Experience

We've already outlined the importance of having a system in place to ensure that you let to the most suitable tenant and can then conduct your duties as a competent Landlord in a compliant and efficient manner. If the truth is told, in reality, even the most compliant and prepared Landlord will have their work cut out when we consider the day-to-day scenarios that will have a bearing on the Tenancy itself. When we consider changes to tenants' circumstances, such as their income and employment, the size and make-up of occupancy, maintenance issues and any external factors, not to mention changes to legislation that then has a direct impact on the running of that tenancy, your experience as a Landlord and ability to constantly evolve and adapt will be crucial. You will need to be aware of the correct procedures to;

- starting a Tenancy (in compliance with the De-Regulation Act 2015),
- collecting and dealing with deposit registrations
- renewing a Tenancy

- 'Novation' of Tenancy
- carrying out routine inspections and what you should be aware of (paying particular attention to the Housing Health and Safety Rating system, the Homes (Fitness for Human Habitation) Act and the Immigration Act)
- dealing with rental arrears
- knowing what you can and can't charge tenants for (in compliance with the Tenant Fee ban)
- serving of notices
- ending a Tenancy
- purchasing a property with a tenant in situ and S3 Notices

...the list is endless!

As a Landlord, you'll need to be prepared to deal with any kind of situation correctly, thus ensuring that you always keep within the parameters of legislative requirements. I've heard numerous horror stories over the years, such as the ways in which private Landlords have set about dealing with rent arrears, ineffective property inspections (or worse still, the absence of them all together!), incorrectly compiled Tenancy documentation including Notices, breaches of Tenancy Deposit legislation, the list goes on! If you thought that the task of a Letting Agent was simply to photocopy pieces of paper, then think again. Your Letting Agency will be tasked with creating and maintaining a system that evolves with changing legislation to ensure that each and every aspect of Tenancy Management is dealt with in such a way that ensures strict compliance at all times.

"Ninety percent of all millionaires become so through owning real estate. More money has been made in real estate than in all industrial investments combined. The wise young man or wage earner of today invests his money in real estate."
- Andrew Carnegie
Billionaire industrialist

KNOW-HOW

So, let's consider in further detail the impact of a reliable and competent Letting Agency and how they can make your life as simplistic as possible when managing your Buy-to-Let investment. Whichever Agent you choose, they will significantly impact your experience as a Landlord. **A good Letting Agent should make your life as a Landlord much easier, but a bad one could put you through a lot of extra stress.**

What Does A Letting Agent Do?

Even if you've given the reins to a letting agent to manage your property, the ultimate responsibility and liability is with you, the Landlord. So, for this reason, it's crucial to choose wisely, but what exactly do Letting Agents do, and what must you consider when searching for the one that's best for you?

It can sometimes take a considerable amount of time to effectively source and secure the most suitable tenant for a rental property, with the potential stress along the way significantly increased due to the legislation's growing complexity with the threat of significant fines for non-compliance. In addition, the impact of the Coronavirus pandemic has also had a bearing on safety measures which have since been implemented, and so as a direct result of this, Letting Agents have had to step up their game, with many overcoming the obstacles they have faced, through investment into industry innovation as demonstrated in the most recent back to work letting agent survey by the Property

Redress Scheme.

The advantages of working with a Letting Agent are very likely to outweigh the expenses if, like many Landlords, you are short on time, perhaps don't live close to your rental property and are not an Industry expert. A knowledgeable Letting Agent should be able to let out your property to a suitable tenant in the shortest time possible and at the highest achievable rent, saving you time, money and hassle.

However, as I mentioned earlier, it's crucial that you make a sensible agency selection, so spend some time researching because there is no such thing as a "let and forget" Landlord. You must choose carefully.

Here, I provide some advice to assist you in finding an agent who will focus on *your* requirements as a Landlord rather than just what's in it for *them*. The relationship should be considered as a partnership whereby you both work to ensure the providing of safe, habitable accommodation whilst also working to ensure the profitability of that investment.

Why use a letting agent:

- Your time is better spent elsewhere
- You would like to have a barrier between you and your tenants, particularly when dealing with any issues that may arise,
- You perhaps don't live within close proximity to your rental property, and you're a new Landlord who isn't fully familiar with the laws governing the private rented sector.
- You prefer to have the assurance that the agent will handle matters in the most efficient manner, thus relieving you of the burden and stress

What enquiries should Landlords be making before selecting a suitable Letting Agent?

Here are some factors to take into account and some questions to ask when comparing agents:

Choosing the right Letting Agent

Below is a list of the typical areas you should consider to help you make that all-important choice. Bear in mind that the cheapest Agent won't necessarily be the best solution and always conduct your own due diligence.

1. Fully Managed Services.

Typically, Letting Agencies will offer a choice of 'Full Tenancy Management' or a 'Let Only' service. The differences between the two are numerous and mainly centred around the level of involvement you will then have once a tenant has been sourced, referenced, and the tenancy has been executed. Now, this is an area that I, as a Letting Agent, feel very strongly about when it comes to deliberating on which is the most suitable for any particular Landlord client. In my honest opinion, knowing the full extent of the complexities of Tenancy management, I firmly believe that it is our duty as responsible Letting Agents to define full tenancy management as a must for any prospective client unless they are a private organisation with a ready-made structure in the background, fully equipped to perform their duties as a Landlord in a totally compliant manner. Yes, I appreciate that this may sound like I have an ulterior motive for such a suggestion, such as the financial gain resulting from ongoing services that we then provide to those clients but in truth, I'm all too aware of the predicaments that many have created for themselves by going it alone. These were seasoned Investors who'd been letting properties for years! For this reason, it will be imperative that the Agency themselves have the 'know-how' and the capability to effectively manage your responsibility as a Landlord. They should be your lifeline, guidance and support, and you should be able to rely upon them accordingly, especially if you live a considerable distance from the property.

2. Analyse nearby letting agents

Make a list of potential Letting Agents once you've determined exactly what it is that they should be providing you with. Examine internet listings, read forum posts, and get advice from other area Landlords. The reputation of Letting Agents is primarily reliant on word of mouth. Ask local Landlords about their experiences working with Letting Agents in your region and have a peek at forum conversations. You may find reviews and ratings on a variety of blogs and websites, including Feefo, Trustpilot and, of course, Google.

A negative experience with a Letting Agent may deter a tenant from prolonging their stay in your rental property or even deter them from renting it in the first place; therefore, it is important to find out how both tenants and Landlords feel about the Agency.

Next, have conversations with the Letting Agents on your shortlist to gauge how they come across. For example, ask them how long it typically takes them to let out a property and whether they have prospective tenants on their books searching for a property similar to yours at that particular time.

3. Ask about fees and look at what agents are offering in exchange for their fees rather than simply selecting an Agency because they are the least expensive.

Price should not be your only consideration when choosing a Letting Agent, but it undoubtedly plays a role.

Although the UK Letting Agent's fees vary, you can

anticipate paying roughly around 10-12% of the monthly rent for a competent and effective full Tenancy Management service. However, this can increase to around 16% depending on the degree of service, the neighbourhood, and which agent you select.

To put the fee into clear context, it is important that you distinguish exactly what the Agent's services entail. Although it may appear so, personally speaking, and knowing the level of work that goes on behind the scenes, I can guarantee you that comparing one Agent to the next is certainly not an 'apples for apples' scenario. Over the years, we have taken over countless tenancies from other Agents and uncovered all kinds of shortcomings through our file audits, such as inventories on two sides of the paper, for example, where ours are typically anywhere between 60 to 100 pages long (specifically to protect both Landlords and tenants when it comes to deposit settlement in the event of a dispute). Another recent example was a property that our Sales department were selling for a client, which was tenanted at the time with a local Letting Agent handling the Tenancy management. As the buyer intended to move into the property, the seller's Letting Agent had served the relevant s21 notice giving his tenants the required two months' notice in which to vacate. On the expiry of that notice, the tenants had not yet sourced onward accommodation, and as such, court intervention was required as is standard practice in such a circumstance. Unfortunately for the seller, however, this appeared to be where the support from his Letting Agent ended, as he was politely informed that he'd have to take care of the remaining procedure himself. As his Selling Agent and with a strong interest in guiding that sale towards completion, naturally, we assisted where we could in advising on the required procedure and likely timescales to regaining vacant possession. To make matters even harder for the client, he was living in Australia at the time. So, the inconvenience of having to handle the remaining procedure was a significant burden on his time and finances, to say the least, all on top of the stress of trying to keep his sale together whilst his buyer applied pressure on the matter to be concluded as he himself had a fast approaching expiry of his mortgage offer! The eventuality was that the seller had ended up having to instruct and pay for a local Solicitor firm to prepare the relevant documentation in order to bring the matter to Court before everything could be successfully concluded. In direct comparison, our own full Tenancy Management service that we provide to our Landlord clients not only covers this procedure from start to finish but also any associated fees such as Court costs, solicitors and bailiff fees, thus giving them complete peace of mind in such situations. In fact, any serious breach of tenancy by the tenant is covered in the same way (non-payment of rent, anti-social behaviour, sub-letting, using the property for illegal or immoral purposes, to name but a few) with protection against non-payment of rent included.

Although it goes without saying that you want good value for your money, a ridiculously low management fee will likely end up costing you more money in the long run when you closely examine the differences between the level of service and what is and isn't included. There is categorically no way that an Agent can go to the full extent of what is required to handle any given situation without having the required infrastructure, which in itself requires the manpower, knowledge and experience as well as ongoing training to keep up with the changing legislation, all of which of course requires continual financial investment which in turn has a direct bearing on their fees.

4. Verify that the agent complies with all legal obligations, including client money protection, membership of a property redress scheme and deposit protection.

It's crucial that you do your homework before selecting a Letting Agency to ensure that they abide by the law.

Property redress scheme membership has been mandatory since 2014, and Landlords should ensure that their Agent is a member of one of the two government schemes (The Property Redress Scheme or The Property Ombudsman). In essence, a redress scheme is a means for the Landlord or tenant to escalate a matter should the Agent not have satisfactorily resolved an issue or complaint.

Since April 2020, Agents should also now be members of a client money protection programme such as 'Client Money Protect' to secure any held clients' funds against misappropriation. As part of the requirements of that membership, Agents must ensure that the relevant certification is prominently displayed in their offices and on their websites. In addition, in accordance with the law, Agents must also ensure that client funds are held in a segregated client account (separate from their own primary bank account) with a bank that the Financial Conduct Authority has approved (FCA) as well as maintaining appropriate professional indemnity insurance.

Under tenancy deposit protection law, any held deposits must be placed in one of the three government-approved schemes (The Deposit Protection Service, Mydeposits or The Dispute Service Limited). A competent Agent will be able to handle the whole process from registering the deposit within the specified timeframe (failure to register within 31 x days of receipt of the deposit will incur a fine to the value of three times the amount of the deposit plus the deposit amount, combined with complications to the regaining of possession of the property), issuing the appropriate documentation to all parties at the specified times as well handling the settlement process at the end of tenancy including negotiations with the tenant on your behalf. The strength of the Inventory and Final Inspection reports are particularly important here (as briefly mentioned earlier) as these will form the basis of your ability to justifiably claim any required amounts and more so in the event that the tenant disagrees with the proposal, leading to the requirement to go through the Alternate

Dispute Resolution process which is an organisation that will then effectively make their own ruling based on the evidence provided by the Agent. Experience in handling such matters is crucial here as the burden of proof is with the Landlord/Agent, so an accurate, detailed report and effective negotiation skills will have a huge bearing on the final outcome.

Membership of an Accreditation Agency such as ARLA, Propertymark, or UKALA is not necessarily a legal requirement; however, from the point of view of a Landlord client, choosing an accredited Agent is perhaps the best way to ensure that you are dealing with a professional Agency that takes their work seriously. As members of UKALA, I know full well the extent of the annual auditing process and the minimum standards we need to meet to maintain that membership.

5. Enquire as to how the agent ensures that the laws governing the private rented sector are followed.

A competent and trustworthy Agency should be completely up to date with all lettings legislation affecting the management of tenancies. There is a multitude of new and current legislation that Letting Agents must be aware of, from the Homes (Fitness for Human Habitation) Act, the Housing Health and Safety Rating System (HHSRS), the Immigration Act, to the Deregulation Act etc. Specifically, with regards to the Homes (Fitness for Human Habitation) Act, Landlords need to ensure that a property is 'fit for human habitation' both at the beginning of the tenancy and throughout and, as such, may be required to make improvements rather than just carry out repairs to reach that required minimum standard. That obligation extends to the dwelling and all parts of the building (including any common or shared areas).

When picking an agent, ask them how they plan to ensure that your property is compliant. For instance, will they make arrangements for a licenced gas engineer to perform the annual gas safety check? Will they ensure that any soft furnishings included in the tenancy abide by fire safety laws? Do they know how to apply the HHSRS and what they should be looking out for? Do they conduct routine inspections, and what do they look out for during each visit? For instance, are they aware of the impact of the Immigration Act (with the potential for criminal prosecution if not followed correctly) when identifying any changes or amendments to those living within the property? Is there an audit trail to each of those inspections (crucial when dealing with possession proceedings)? Although the Landlord still has the legal obligation for following the law, a skilled agent will be able to provide advice on all of these areas and more.

6. What advertising techniques will the agent use to promote your rental property in order to attract the most suitable tenants at the highest rent possible?

Verify that the Letting Agent will employ a variety of tactics to source tenants for your property and that they have a proactive marketing approach.

To determine whether they effectively market rental properties and whether they've recently successfully let out numerous properties in your neighbourhood, check out their property listings on a property portal like Rightmove.

Do they make full use of social media with featured and sponsored ads to reach specifically targeted audiences through certain demographics? What is the quality of their marketing particulars like, such as the use of professional photography with a wide angle lens to capture the whole room and to focus on presenting properties in the best possible light (quite literally) and investment into the use of 3D Virtual Tours (which have shown to increase online engagement by as much as 368% as well as then enabling digital viewings to prospective tenants where immediate access to the property is perhaps hindered by existing tenants requiring sufficient notice)? What other forms of marketing and advertising do they carry out, and how prominently do they appear to the tenant market as an agent? Do they command attention and possess a thorough knowledge of the local neighbourhood? To see how they market their properties and how effective they are at letting out properties in that specific area, make sure they have listings on the main internet portals. Use that opportunity to review the quality of the photography and how appealing those properties appear to you (if they don't jump out at you, then they also won't be appealing to the prospective tenant.

7. Has the agent adopted technology and flexible working techniques in order to adapt to the "new normal"?

Letting Agents were compelled to change their procedures during the lockdown. Many did so successfully by utilising technology to allow for virtual viewings (as mentioned earlier) and even virtual inspections. It's important to find out how they adjusted to the changes brought on by the coronavirus pandemic, as those who displayed adaptability and toughness in these challenging times may be better equipped to withstand future storms.

The Property Redress Scheme's recent Back to work Letting Agent survey reveals some of the ways that Letting Agents have adjusted and that many plan to provide their clients with the advantages of flexible working arrangements and new technologies adopted during the lockdown as they adjust to the **"new normal."**

8. Does the agent have market knowledge in the area?

In most cases, selecting a Letting Agency that works in the same neighbourhood as your rental property makes appropriate sense. When trying to convince tenants of the advantages of a property, such as its close proximity to quality schools and transportation options, local knowledge is crucial.

A local agent will also be better equipped to handle any maintenance difficulties because they are more likely to have a solid network of professional contacts, including plumbers and electricians. Visit the agents' offices to learn more about them and their familiarity with the neighbourhood.

They should be able to advise you on matters like establishing your rent at the most appropriate amount and how to bring that property up to code, as they'll understand how to entice the most suitable tenants.

A long-established agent is also considerably less likely to experience financial difficulties than one who has just started their business.

9. Enquire about your prospective union.

Last but not least, confirm that you are satisfied with the letting agent's treatment of you as a client. A few things are worth double-checking as follows

- Operating times

Some letting agents only operate during normal business hours on weekdays, which could present a problem for both you as a Landlord and for current and potential tenants. Enquire about the agency's availability at the weekends and in the evenings.

- Paperwork

Ask the Letting Agency how they will handle rental-related documents, such as tenancy agreements, references, and credit and employment checks. Will they, for instance, allow you to check any references they have for potential tenants? They may do this legally if they obtain the tenants' consent.

- Alterations and upkeep

If you've decided to utilise a management agency, ask the letting agent how frequently they inspect the property, how the tenants may get in touch with them in case of a maintenance issue, and whether they have a list of reliable contractors they work with.

- Transfers of funds

Ask the letting agent how they will handle the money associated with the rental, including the rent collected and associated charges and fees. Ask them how frequently they will transfer funds to your account and the timescale from the rent collection from the tenant to payment to you. Notice intervals.

To know what will happen if you decide to end the connection, it is crucial to learn how long the Letting Agent's notice period is. Most Letting Agents need three months' written notice before terminating a Management Agreement.

Steps to take after selecting a Letting Agent

When you've found the ideal Letting Agent, read the Agency Agreement before signing it. Examine the fees and the termination provisions in particular.

Also, make sure that the Letting Agent provides you with copies of the signed tenancy agreement and any other important paperwork. They should also give you copies of receipts or invoices for any work that they organise.

Make sure the Agency Agreement is crystal clear and that it outlines what the Agent has committed to do for you, when they will do it, and how they will do it.

The significance of being diligent

As we've seen, selecting a Letting Agency is a complicated process with many factors to consider. As a result, it may be tempting for a busy Landlord to engage the services of the first one they come across rather than spending important time looking through various options.

Landlords tend not to conduct adequate due diligence on the Agents they enquire with, despite the fact that the quality of their chosen Agency can determine whether or not a let will be successful.

Remember also that it is not just the relationship between you and the Agency that you need to consider but also the relationship between the Agency and the tenant. A happy tenant is a happy Landlord, so by looking out for the interest of your tenant, the Agent will also be looking out for yours.

"You will come to know that what appears today to be a sacrifice will prove instead to be the greatest investment that you will ever make."
– Gordon B. Hickey

PRESERVATION
MANAGEMENT OF PROPERTY

For a number of reasons, it's crucial for a Landlord to maintain their property to a decent level, such as giving tenants a safe, habitable living space (to which they are legally entitled), lowering the number of pricey repairs that they may have to make over time and to maintain its value.

The latter is crucial if you ever decide to sell the property in the future and want to maximise your return on investment.

Any decent Lettings Agency should consider the above factors while they work to preserve and maintain your property asset and maximise that investment. So here are some top suggestions for maintaining the property's condition, keeping the overall value in mind.

- Take firm action.

Whilst it may be tempting to delay rectifying maintenance issues and general improvements or even ignore the problem completely to save money, issues like wetness, mould and broken gutters won't go away on their own and will probably end up costing much more to fix if immediate action isn't taken (think of the saying 'a stitch in time saves nine').

- Don't go with the cheapest works

It's never a good idea to skimp on quality and pay less for poor or subpar service, but that doesn't mean you have to spend a lot of money. Just be open-minded to the fact that reliable tradespeople will undoubtedly cost a little more than your 'run of the mill' contractor, whose skill level may not be sufficient, and their availability may not be so accommodating, potentially leaving your tenant exposed to the reported issues for longer. Decent Lettings Agencies will have likely built up solid relationships with a variety of contractors enabling them to be able to rely upon greater flexibility and responsiveness whilst attending to reported maintenance issues (in certain cases, Agents' work is prioritised over their own, due to the level of business that they may receive). Additionally, they'll be in the position to be able to coordinate works from start to finish, including handling access via the tenants, follow-ups if problems re-occur etc.

- Service frequently.

To ensure that your stoves and boilers are operating efficiently, pay particular attention to having a contractor perform regular maintenance on them. That action alone can significantly lower the likelihood of anything going wrong in the future.

- Spend time and money on it.

You must set aside enough time and be prepared to make monthly maintenance payments to keep the property in good condition, thus saving money over time. In addition, I would recommend saving up three months' worth of rent to cover void periods or emergencies. It's also crucial to keep in mind that older homes typically demand more upkeep.

Ensure you carry out regular inspections.

The property should be periodically inspected to ensure that the general upkeep is sufficient. In addition, those routine inspections will enable you to get a solid understanding of the property's condition, thus allowing you to carry out preventative maintenance as necessary.

A recent legal modification:

Since the Homes (Fitness for Human Habitation) Act was

enacted in 2019, keeping a property in the right condition has become even more important for Landlords. The Act specifies that all rented accommodation should be suitable for human habitation. It increases tenants' rights to legal action against the few Landlords who disregard their duty to maintain their properties accordingly.

It changed the Landlord and Tenant Act of 1985 to mandate that all Landlords should maintain their properties in a condition suitable for habitation both at the start of the tenancy and throughout. By giving tenants the ability to take legal action against their Landlords should they feel that the property has been poorly maintained, the government's aim was to raise the standards in the private rental sector. Prior to the passing of this piece of legislation, tenants were dependent on their local government to hold their Landlord accountable, whereas now, the path of action that they can take is far more simplified and direct.

For a number of reasons, a property could be judged unfit for human habitation, including the following:

- Drainage issues and issues with the availability of hot and cold water.
- Issues including dampness, crowding, and inadequate ventilation.
- Weak structural integrity or unsound design.
- A poorly maintained or neglected property.
- Little natural light, room to prepare and cook food, or space to clean up.

In addition, the courts may rule that a property is unfit for habitation if it has any of the 29 hazards listed in the Housing Health and Safety Rating System (England) 2005.

On the other hand, there are a number of circumstances in which you won't be held accountable for an unfit home, including problems brought on by acts of God (such as fires, storms, and floods) or situations in which the tenants' own possessions or behaviour have caused the issue.

Repairs and Section 21

A Landlord who disregards the specified and time-limited repair process may invalidate a Section 21 notice and prohibit one from being served for a period of six months, according to revisions to Section 21 notifications that came into effect on October 1, 2018.

(At the time of writing, the Government's White Paper proposes to drastically reform the private rented sector and, amongst the proposals, aims to remove the s21 Notice completely).

It has always been a Landlord's duty to maintain a rental property in good condition, ensuring all electrical, heating, and plumbing systems are in working order. However, since recent new laws around retaliatory evictions in England have been brought in, it's now even more important that reported maintenance issues by tenants are attended to and dealt with in an appropriate time and manner. Failure to do so will likely complicate the process of regaining possession if ever required.

There are certain guidelines that you must work to, and although there isn't a complete list from that which is a Landlord's responsibility to that of a tenant's, you are required to respond "fairly" which can, of course, be ambiguous.

I would advise you always to follow the rule of caution and attempt to do more than what is required to demonstrate that you exercised due diligence and took reasonable precautions to keep the property and your tenants safe and secure.

What are the duties regarding property maintenance for a Landlord?

For any rental property you own, you should establish a maintenance schedule outlining what needs to be done and when, especially regarding electrical and gas appliances.

- A Gas Safe registered engineer (http://www.gassaferegister.co.uk) is required to perform an annual gas safety check, and your tenants must be given all copies as and when.
- A "Part P" registered electrician should inspect the electrical installation at least once every five years as part of an 'Electrical Installation Condition Report'.
- Ensure that you perform a fire safety risk assessment. It is advisable to enlist the services of a fire safety expert, which your Letting Agent can arrange for you.
- Keep a record of the dates on which smoke detectors, heat sensors, and carbon monoxide detectors have been inspected. Additionally, you must conduct a legionella examination to demonstrate your evaluation of the possibility that stagnant water may contain the deadly bacterium.

A thorough tenancy agreement should specify exactly what you, as a Landlord, are accountable for maintaining and what the tenant should be responsible for in terms of general maintenance.

The tenant should be responsible for maintaining the property in a good state and refrain from doing anything that would cause damage or deterioration beyond what would be considered reasonable wear and tear. Tenants are often responsible for performing smaller tasks like changing light bulbs and maintaining clear plugholes. In addition, they must notify the Landlord of any issues, such as leaks, that need to be fixed urgently.

In many circumstances, the Landlord's duty is to maintain the building's roof, floor slabs, walls, windows, and doors, as well as the pruning of trees and shrubs and the safety of the building's pathways.

It's crucial to keep in mind that your Landlord insurance will probably include a "Reasonable Precautions" clause. The tenant is required to take all reasonable steps to prevent or minimise loss, destruction, damage, accident or injury and preserve the premises, machinery, equipment and furniture to a good state of repair," according to the tenancy.

Therefore, it will probably imply that the property needs to be kept free of any hazards or threats, such as by making sure:

All portable electrical appliances are in working order and are kept in a safe state, and the gutters and drains are clear. The bannisters are fixed and not loose; the inside flooring is in good condition and not a trip hazard. It's in your best interest to maintain as much of that as you can, as relying too much on the tenant won't help if and when it comes to making an insurance claim.

What legal duties do Landlords have to do during repairs to their properties?

There shouldn't be many unforeseen repairs if your maintenance programme is being followed. However, should something need fixing, your Agent should make plans to have it examined and have any repairs made as soon as feasible.

Additionally, you need to be aware of the MEES regulations (Minimum Energy Efficiency Standards) and how they affect your rental property. Since April 2020, the minimum EPC rating in order to be able to let out a property is E; however, from 2025, this will be reduced to a C, so it is important to start making arrangements now in terms of the works required in order to increase energy efficiency sufficiently.

The property's utilities must be in good working condition, ensuring the tenants can heat them adequately and keep them risk-free. Any necessary repairs must be made as soon as feasible for moisture, heat, and safety, and tenants' concerns must, at the very least, be replied to within 14 days of receiving their contact.

You could be charged and/or fined if you don't, and your tenant subsequently complains to the council.

Understanding the retaliatory eviction provision that was enacted as part of the Deregulation Act is crucial. Landlords will not be able to enforce a Section 21 notice to evict tenants if it is determined that they failed to make the required repairs after that tenant filed a formal complaint about the state of the property.

Therefore, to protect oneself in case the situation worsens, it is very much in your interest as a Landlord to act swiftly and ensure you have a thorough written record of all communications with your tenant. For this reason, a decent Lettings Agency will maintain a thorough written record of the timeline of all events throughout a tenancy.

How quickly is a Landlord required to attend to maintenance issues?

Maintenance should be addressed and rectified in a "reasonable" amount of time. Therefore, I would advise that any issue be dealt with or responded to within 24 hours of it being reported or slightly longer if not classed as an emergency.

Tenants can occasionally fail to appreciate that Landlords don't have a magic hotline to contractors and therefore aren't always accessible. So when responding to maintenance issues, it is important to manage their expectations by sending contractors as soon as possible and letting them know that it may take a few days before any work is completed. Again, communication here is key, and again, a competent and professional Lettings Agency will skilfully manage any such situation, maintaining harmony within the Landlord and tenant relationship.

More specifically, as part of our own Tenancy Management service, tenants of our Landlord clients' properties are able to make use of our 'online maintenance reporting platform' 24/7, whereby they then have direct access to our response team (even outside of normal working hours) enabling issues to be dealt with in a timely and efficient manner. As part of that system, we also provide advice to tenants for simple fixes, minimising where possible the need for a contractor call out, thus saving costs to the Landlord. Generally speaking, around 25% of maintenance issues reported via this system are resolved online and without the use of a contractor!

Should Landlords notify tenants in writing when there are repairs to be made?

Although communicating with tenants in writing has always been a good idea, the new retaliatory eviction rule makes it much more important that Landlords preserve records. Nowadays, sending an email asking for a "read receipt" should serve instead of posting or delivering a letter. However, if a phone discussion has occurred, it is always wise to follow it up in writing.

Keep in mind that tenants must be given at least 24 hours' notice before anyone can enter the property unless for an emergency. I would always suggest contacting by phone and email, outlining the planned work and providing information about the contractor who will be present.

Can Landlords impose repair fees on tenants?

The simplest response is no unless the tenants themselves were responsible for the damage, which should be clear from the check-in inventory report. Since the Landlord is responsible for maintenance and repairs, they must pay for them.

Can tenants withhold rent for maintenance?

There is never a circumstance in which a tenant has the right to withhold rent, as specified within the signed Tenancy Agreement, as it is regarded as unconnected to any problems they might be experiencing.

They must follow the necessary legal procedures if they have any issues regarding the property's condition, your communication (or lack thereof), or anything else. You might be able to evict your tenant if they merely cease paying their rent unless they can show you weren't as responsible as you should have been, in which case an eviction will be challenging.

Are the costs of repairs and maintenance for a rental property tax deductible?

You should get assistance from a qualified property tax practitioner because property tax is a complicated and specialised field. For example, your maintenance and repair expenses can generally be written off, but anything deemed an improvement cannot.

The best advice is to work with a bookkeeper and/or accountant who has long-term experience with real estate investment clients. Also, get an account from someone who invests themselves because they have a personal interest in staying current with changes.

Can I acquire maintenance insurance for my rental property?

The majority of general maintenance is not covered by insurance because "wear and tear" is a natural component of owning property. You can, however, obtain coverage for specific problems, such as boiler breakdowns, that could necessitate costly repairs.

As a Landlord, it's reasonable that you might be unaware of what upkeep is necessary to make sure your home complies with all applicable laws and the housing health and safety rating system requirements (HHSRS). So it's worthwhile getting in touch with your local council housing department and requesting someone come out to the property to advise you.

The most important thing to keep in mind is that performing repairs and maintenance correctly and frequently is better for your property and your wallet. In addition, quick fixes encourage tenants to stay longer and care for your property better, leading to fewer general repairs, void periods, and more punctual rent payments. As the saying goes, if you take care of your property, it will take care of you.

What additional expenses would I have as a Landlord?

A property's upkeep might be expensive. To prevent smaller, more frequent chores from growing larger and more costly, it pays to stay on top of them. In addition to letting and management costs, Landlords should take the following into account:

- Repairs
- Exterior upkeep, such as window washing and landscaping
- Landlord insurance
- Renovation and décor
- Cleaning costs
- Tax on any profits made from rental revenue
- Loss of rent from a void period

Understandably, Landlords will find it difficult to stay current with the buy-to-let legislation and regulations, which are continually changing. For those with far-flung properties, limited industry knowledge, or a sizable portfolio to manage, a lettings and management agent's services may be absolutely necessary.

For Landlords, the temptation to cut costs and go it alone exists; however, my recommendation is to always seek expert assistance as long-term, it will be well worth it, especially if you work with a trustworthy agent who is supportive of your buy-to-let investment.

"Time is more valuable than money. You can get more money, but you cannot get more time."
— Jim Rohn
American success coach and philosopher

INHABITANT

Undoubtedly, one of the most crucial stages to ensuring a successful tenancy is the quality of the sourcing and vetting of potential tenants. At this part of the proceedings, it can be make or break as you attempt to generate interest from those you deem most suitable and worthy of your consideration. Factors to consider whilst filtering through the list of prospective tenants are;

- How you intend to verify the source and amount of their monthly or overall income, as well as establishing what rent-to-income ratio you should be measuring against,
- Whether a guarantor is required and how their suitability should be assessed,
- Establishing the number of occupants that there will be within the household and their relationship to each other to determine then the suitability of the property based on its size, location and set up of neighbouring properties,
- The likely timescale that they would require the property for and whether that matches your own requirements,
- Their 'right to rent' status in the UK,
- Their credit score, whether there are any County Court Judgments or Individual Voluntary Arrangements with creditors and how you should deal will such circumstances,
- Your preferences to pets and smokers,

- The suitability of references from previous Landlords,

The more consideration that there is during the preliminary stages, the more likely you are to achieve harmony within the Landlord and tenant relationship.

From the onset, the strength of that relationship will be dependent on clear communication between you and your tenant, which in itself highlights the importance of a professionally written tenancy agreement (of which there are several different types) that outlines the specific terms and responsibilities for both parties in order to create and maintain the fairness and balance that is required to ensure that the Agreement is legally enforceable. In addition, understanding the differences between the different types of tenancies is essential to ensure you're relying on the right one, depending on the type of property set-up you have or the tenancy arrangement you are dealing with.

Checklist for tenancy agreements

A tenancy should, as a minimum, include the following clauses:

- The tenancy's start date and minimum fixed term,
- The basis of how the tenancy will be renewed and what the default will be if a renewal is not signed by either party and notice is not given by either side,
- Details of significant interior and exterior fixtures, as well as an addendum containing the items listed in the inventory,
- Information on the amount of the deposit and details of the Deposit Protection scheme where it will be held, together with the scheme's contact details,
- The agreed rental amount when it's due, how it should be paid, and what will happen if not paid in a

timely manner,

- The terms in which possession of the property can be reclaimed, together with the relevant notice requirements,
- Tenants' responsibilities include maintaining the property to the appropriate condition and informing the Landlord or agent of any issues that require attention,
- A definition of "fair wear and tear," emphasising how some components of the property, such as carpets, may naturally deteriorate with time and how that should be treated,
- the tenant's and Landlord's signatures (s)

Setting up a tenancy

As already mentioned briefly, there are different types of tenancy agreements dependent on the circumstances of the let, and your Letting Agent should be well-positioned to understand which you will require and when.

Tenancy types

The most commonly used is an Assured Shorthold Tenancy (AST), but others available are;

- Excluded tenancy (lodging)
- Assured tenancy
- Non-assured tenancy
- Regulated tenancy
- Company let

Assured shorthold tenancy

The majority of tenancies are ASTs by default, particularly where the property is a private residence (not commercial), the tenancy began after 1989, the property serves as the tenant's primary residence, and you, the Landlord, do not reside there.

You can even use an AST when letting out individual rooms to tenants who share facilities.

Circumstances where an AST may not be suitable could be where rent exceeds £100k per year, low or no rent, or for holiday lets.

The majority of assured shorthold tenancy agreements include a predetermined initial term of say six or twelve months for example and unless the tenant agrees or there is a rent review clause inserted, the rental amount cannot be increased during that term. The Tenancy Agreement automatically crosses to a periodic tenancy if no further fixed term is entered into. A word of warning here, you should make absolutely certain that you insert a clause that states that without a new fixed-term being entered into, the default is that it becomes a 'contractual periodic tenancy'. Unless this clause is specifically inserted, your AST will become a 'statutory periodic tenancy', which you absolutely want to avoid for the following reasons. Part of your tenant's responsibility will be to pay all utility bills such as gas, electric, water and council tax. With specific reference to council tax, should your AST become a 'statutory periodic tenancy' and then, during that time, the tenant fails to pay it for whatever reason, the Local Authority may well be able to hold you responsible for that amount (Leeds City Council V Broadley (2016)) as technically, an SPT is a new Tenancy Agreement, and with any Tenancy with a term of less than 6 x months, the Landlord cannot pass the responsibility of council tax to the tenant! A CPT is a continuation and extension of the existing tenancy on a monthly basis and so not classed as a new tenancy, so the original Agreement is still in place.

Non-assured shorthold tenancy

Only in specific circumstances, where an assured shorthold tenancy cannot be employed, may this type of tenancy be used. This might be the case if the monthly rent is less than £250pcm, the tenant has a primary residence elsewhere, or you share a residence with your tenant (so long as you don't share any amenities) with them.

You are not required to submit the deposit into a government-backed deposit protection scheme or provide a Section 21 or Section 8 Notice to end the tenancy because this is not an assured shorthold tenancy. As long as the tenant abides by the conditions of the tenancy agreement, then they have the right to remain in the property until the end of the defined period.

Excluded tenancy (for lodgers)

An excluded tenancy may exist if you cohabitate on the property with your tenant and share amenities (for instance, if you host a lodger). As opposed to an assured shorthold tenancy, excluded tenancies don't offer the tenant as many protections. However, as long as you follow the terms of the tenancy agreement, you are not required to place any held deposit in one of the government-approved deposit schemes and are typically able to remove the tenant without a court order and without the need to give notice.

Company let

This is a 'Non-Housing Act' Agreement and is not bound by the laws created by the Housing Act, such as deposit registration, the Tenant Fee ban and s21 notices. As such, the deposit does not need to be registered with any of the schemes; you are legally entitled to charge fees for administration, etc. In terms of regaining possession, you would simply be required to issue a 'Notice to Quit'. You would use this type of Agreement if the tenant is a company that intends to house employees of that company during the tenancy term. They are able to change and modify the household as frequently as they require, as the tenancy will always be in the company's name rather than those of the occupants. One important point to distinguish here is that a company that lets a property with the intention of then subletting to tenants such as on a 'serviced accommodation' basis is NOT the grounds for entering into a Company Tenancy Agreement. Over the years and with the growing in popularity of serviced accommodation, I have had numerous conversations with individuals within such companies who perceive this kind of setup to be applicable to a Company Agreement and therefore see nothing wrong with one being used as the basis of them then carrying out their intended activity by subletting. If you should find yourself in such a situation, then technically, your tenant (the Company) is breaching the terms of that Agreement by subletting. Still more so, this may also cause issues when it comes to regaining possession, as well as complications with the terms of your mortgage (if there is one) and buildings insurance. The correct setup here is to have a 'Management Agreement' in place with that company, who then operates with their own appropriate Tenancy Agreement with their specific tenants.

Security for deposits

We've already discussed the procedure with regards to collecting and registering deposits which is extremely important to ensure you keep within the terms of the Deregulation Act.

The tenant should be given a copy of the Deposit registration certificate attesting to the total amount that has been secured and followed up with a duplicate copy at the point of any tenancy renewal.

Inventories

The Inventory's quality, detail and thoroughness is extremely important when it comes to ensuring that the condition of the property when you get it back at the end of the tenancy is acceptable. I briefly mentioned earlier how my company's own 'check in' and 'check out' procedures are incredibly detailed for this specific reason. Clearly, the level of detail required to carry this out to a professional standard will cost time and money. So all too often, I've seen situations where Landlords settle for a below-standard inventory report or, worse still, the absence of one altogether, with the intention of saving an expense, just because the property was unfurnished, as they believed that there was nothing that could potentially be damaged or removed. Consider then the impact of damaged walls, broken windows, dirty kitchens and bathrooms, overgrown and poorly kept gardens, items of old furniture and junk left behind, not to mention intentional damage or destruction of the Landlord's property. I'm not putting together a list intended to put you off letting out the property. I'm merely outlining what may require rectification before you could even consider remarketing a property to find new prospective tenants. Yet, the Landlord, whose opinion is that if a property is unfurnished, then an inventory is not required, will have failed to consider any of these scenarios. Worse still, they would now be faced with a situation where they have no chance of claiming from the deposit as they have no documented proof of the condition of the property from the onset, left to cover the cost of works from their own pocket!

The bottom line, a reputable Letting Agency will understand the importance of a solid process, not just of the structure and detail of the Inventory or Final Inspection reports but also the level of skill required to mediate on the deposit settlement, avoiding conflict and disagreement between the parties wherever possible. A mishandled or poorly conducted 'check in' and 'check out' process is likely to develop into larger and more costly problems as you go from tenancy to tenancy as each new Inventory report with the 'check in' of a new tenant will then document the property in a more dilapidated state. This would then undoubtedly create allowances for that new tenant to hand the property back in a similar or worse condition, as the property's condition from the onset was far from ideal. Sticking with this particular point, this is specifically the reason why I would always encourage a Landlord to invest money into a property prior to letting it out (such as new carpets, repaint, new kitchen and bathroom etc.) so that the condition is such that clearly sets the standard of what is expected in terms of how it should be left. Moreso, the Landlord is more likely to attract the better quality tenant, who is more likely to treat the property with the care and consideration that we would expect or hope for. Therefore, investing a little money now saves a lot of expenses in the future.

Deposit settlement and the dealing of any related disputes at the end of a tenancy

So following on from the 'check out' process, if the tenant has adhered to the conditions of the Tenancy Agreement, including payment of rent and utility bills, they should be entitled to receive their deposit without any deductions. If, on the other hand, the tenant has violated any of the terms, then there may be a requirement to make a claim against it.

As a best practice, towards the end of tenancy and before the tenant vacates, the Landlord should encourage the tenant to attend to any required cleaning, paying particular attention to the original inventory as a benchmark for the minimum required standard.

Following the 'check out' report, there are ten days within which the deposit should be returned, assuming no works are required.

Suppose works that the tenant should be considered responsible for are identified. In that case, there is the opportunity for the case to be referred to the Alternate Dispute Resolution service should an agreement between the parties not be achievable. Clearly, this would be a scenario better avoided as the initial cost to bring the property up to scratch and in a suitable condition for the next tenant would then likely have to be met by the Landlord initially, whose interest would be to avoid a drawn-out void period until a decision is made and funds distributed. Once again, this highlights the importance of an effective and competent Lettings Agency that will continually work to establish and maintain the harmony between Landlord and tenant, ensuring that the processes are as effective and efficient as required, thus increasing the chances of a smooth transition from tenancy to tenancy.

Evictions and ending leases

The initial term of a tenancy agreement is most commonly either 6 or 12 months, after which point it would either be renewed onto a new fixed term or would roll onto a periodic tenancy, assuming that neither the Landlord nor tenant has given the required notice to end the tenancy altogether. The notice required by the Landlord is a s21 Form 6a and, importantly, must be served correctly. If you're within the 1st tenancy term, then that notice cannot be served until at least four months have passed; however, from any renewal tenancy onwards, it can be served at any point. In the case of a breach of tenancy by the tenant, the process changes considerably. The required notice would be a s8, and the relevant grounds relied upon would be dependent on the nature of the breach, i.e. rent arrears, anti-social behaviour, sub-letting, using the property for illegal or immoral purposes etc. Many consider the s21 notice to be the more simplified process to regaining possession, even in the event of a breach of tenancy. Still, nothing stops you from serving both for added security.

KEY TAKEAWAYS

- With over 170 pieces of legislation that govern the private rental sector, the last thing any Landlord should want is a 'watered down' service with the Agent forced to cut corners due to financial restraints,
- Above all, the Agent needs to mitigate the risks of letting property which can be in abundance when a Tenancy is not managed correctly
- The biggest concern for any Landlord when letting out their property is whether they will attract the best quality tenant who will pay their rent promptly and look after the property to the level expected. However, not every Landlord understands the principles behind achieving this in terms of how the property should be maintained in order to attract and keep the right tenant in the first place.
- It is important for the Landlord to have a system in place to monitor every aspect of the Tenancy in terms of rent payments, reported maintenance issues, an audit trail to document all reported maintenance and, therefore, evidence of resolution of it,
- A Landlord /Tenant relationship can be a delicate one at the best of times. There can often be a perception in the Tenant's mind that Landlords are greedy, unsympathetic and inconsiderate individuals who are more with their pocket rather than the needs and requirements of their tenants. So when it comes to maintenance issues or general investing back into the property to make it more appealing and pleasant, there is little to no interest. Part of the essential role of a competent Lettings Agency is to ensure that this relationship is managed just as well as the property/Tenancy is. There should be transparency and fairness on both sides as, of course, both

Landlord and Tenant have obligations to adhere to via the terms of the Tenancy Agreement

- Maintenance issues should be dealt with in a timely and efficient manner
- A thorough Inventory and 'check out' process should be in place to ensure that should there be any damage outside of general wear and tear, that the process of claiming from the Tenant's deposit is not hindered or complicated.
- Rent ledgers should be well managed, and more so, in the event of rent arrears, the process for following up should not contravene any of the tenants' rights, and so therefore, the Agent should be careful not to do or cause any issues which would give the right to the Tenant to claim against the Landlord.
- Any notices should be served in accordance with the legislation to ensure their effectiveness, and more so, as part of the Deregulation Act, all Landlord prescribed information should be documented as being served to the Tenant at the relevant times as will be required to be demonstrated at the point of bringing any case to Court when seeking possession
- Deposits must be registered in accordance with Deposit Protection legislation so as to avoid financial penalties as well as hindering the process of regaining possession
- All certifications (Gas Safety Certs, Electrical Installation Condition Reports and Legionella tests) must be carried out at the relevant times. Again, there must be a full audit trail,
- In the case of HMOs, all Tenants MUST have an 'out of hours' maintenance contact
- In the case of a 5x bed or more HMO, inspections must be carried out weekly to comply with the HMO Fire Safety Regs
- The Agent should keep the Landlord client up to date with any changes to legislation that impact them or

the property, as well as assuring them that they are taking care of everything necessary to ensure compliance at all times

- As the Agent is the eyes and ears to the Landlord, they should ensure that they are acting in their best interests in working towards maintaining the property to a satisfactory standard, maintaining the Landlord /Tenant relationship, ensuring that an efficient process of maintenance management is in place at all times and that all legislation is adhered to so that the safety of the Tenant is never compromised.

- The Landlord invests into property as a financial asset and therefore requires that asset to perform at the required level to make the most on that ROI. The Agent should therefore assist in helping to ensure that those levels are not negatively affected by poor management service. The Agent should be attentive to anything that would have a bearing on that, be that Tenant behaviour or general maintenance etc

*"Cheap agents aren't great,
and great agents aren't cheap!
Offering low fees should not be
the basis for securing new
instructions from landlord clients
but rather the quality and
effectiveness of service offered
in return
for the fee charged."
– Vittorio G Fierro*

⊲◆⊳

*"Price is what you pay.
Value is what you get."
– Warren Buffet*

Conclusion

So there you have it, my complete 'Time Tested and Proven Property Investment Profit System'. I sincerely hope that it has helped you to understand and appreciate all of the components that go into property investment and, more importantly, successful property investment. As explained in detail through the chapters, with the correct approach, careful consideration and planning, it is possible to create, build and sustain a high-performing property portfolio that generates the return on investment that you require and with an open mind to the importance of thorough and efficient tenancy management; you will have a system whereby you're well equipped and prepared to deal with any possible eventuality. Let's be honest, life is far from perfect and full of surprises, and this is no more true when it comes to managing a portfolio of tenancies. It is important to remember that you're not just dealing with assets (properties) but also people, and so with the impact of their own changing circumstances in their own lives, this may also then have a bearing on you and the tenancy itself. You may have found the perfect tenant, conducted thorough references, set up the tenancy, and everything is going according to plan until all of a sudden, things change for the worse for whatever reason leading then to issues such as rent arrears or any other such breach of tenancy. I can tell you now that I've seen many examples of this over the years, but pointing a finger of blame at anyone, in particular, will change nothing. Nobody can completely eradicate such a scenario, but anyone can have a system that ensures that effective and efficient systems are in place to cope and deal with any such matter, whether that be getting a tenancy back in order or successfully regaining possession to then start again. Believe me, managing a tenancy that's going well is hard enough but managing one where there may be complications for whatever reason takes every ounce of your capability and character. Those who decide to cut corners or are not astute to the changing horizon will undoubtedly open themselves up to greater problems along the way.

Your investment into property will have come from hard work and determination, so you owe it to yourself to ensure you get the best out of this opportunity. The clever, well-prepared investor, whether on their own or with the help, guidance and assistance from a competent and reputable property professional, will undoubtedly succeed in creating the financial freedom they desire. On the other hand, the short-sighted Investor, ill-prepared for any possible eventuality, will likely succumb to the financial stresses that can result from poorly made decisions or lack of experience, especially in tenancy management. The question is, which one are you going to be?

I wish you well in your property investment journey, and I'm on hand to help and assist wherever I can.

Vittorio G Fierro BA (Hons)

LinkedIn profile URL: www.linkedin.com/in/vito-fierro
Email add: vitof@cityandcounty.net
Company URL: www.cityandcounty.net

Testimonials

Vittorio G Fierro is a real Italian stallion, very unassuming when you first meet him but quietly confident. A real perfectionist by nature, and when he puts his mind to something... consider that thing done!

The birth of this book, "Property Investment Mastery", was no exception for Vito (as he likes to be called by friends and family members).

I first met Vito at one of Sally Lawson's legendary Agent Rainmaker Bootcamps in January 2019.

I work closely with her to help her clients with their Mindset and Public Speaking. Vito was then selected as one of Sally's speakers at her annual, "AgentRainmaker Live event in October 2019 of the same year.

I coached Vito to speak on stage. He was amazing on the day, and his performance was one of the best at the ARLIVE2019 event. He was a natural-born speaker. He just needed to learn the skills.

From that experience, he then asked me to provide ongoing coaching in the Art of Public Speaking and it was during one of our coaching sessions that the idea of writing a book was born. The rest, as they say, was history.

Vito has put all of his 24 years of experience in the property industry into this book (Property Investment Mastery). It's a bulletproof property investment framework for those serious about property investing to reap maximum rewards in return.

This book is a must-read for all property investors and those aspiring to get into property investing as well.

Vito, thank you for sharing your knowledge and know-how with the rest of the world.

Tosin Ogunnusi -

"International Empowerment Trainer & Executive Coach." Author of 3 Best Selling Books "Time 2 Break Free" "Empower Yourself with 7 Natural Laws" & "Perform Like A Champion Every Time You Speak"

Vito is one of those people you meet who you know is true to his core values of delivering high-level value to anyone he meets; now at the helm of his family business spanning 40 plus years of trade, he has been assisting people with buying, selling and letting properties throughout three recessions, global downturns and rises and throughout all of that, remained loyal to his clients and delivering great service.

In relation to buying properties for investment, he carries the same loyal values, and he has more experience than many, so, therefore, he knows a good or a bad deal when he sees it—a great read for any investor looking to learn from one of the true property professionals out there.

Sally Lawson
*_Former ARLA President (2017/2018), Real Estate, Letting Agency and Marketing Specialist_*

Printed in Great Britain
by Amazon

17019983R00078